LOCUS

You Too Can Understand–
The East Asian Financial Crisis

Sayling Wen

Illustrated by Chih-Chung Tsai
Translated from Chinese by Jonathan Ross

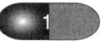

The Declaration of Tomorrow Studio

Human beings are what make the changes and advances of history possible. Creation, destruction, success, and failure all come from man and man's actions. It is in man's nature to challenge limits and strive for a better future.

It is our belief that all human beings share the dream and hope to free themselves from the narrowness of individualism, blood relationship, and regionalism so that they can travel freely in time and space to create a better future. And this belief is why a great number of elite people join hands to form a professional writers' group - Tomorrow Studio. All of us in Tomorrow Studio expect to contribute good books to foster the dream and to benefit the future of human beings.

There are two definitions of "ming-ri" (literally bright day.)

One is simply "tomorrow." Future dreams and

goals sound very remote; yet tomorrow seems more real and more tangible. If we want to create a better tomorrow, we should start today.

The other definition of "ming-ri" is "to know what is intended for oneself and to be a new person every day."

To know what is intended for oneself is to know the past and the future; to know ethics, civilization, and the rules of the world; to have ideals and goals. It is to utilize human beings' property - our accumulated knowledge and collected wisdom - and to abide by the moral standards long established.

To be a new person every day is to rid oneself of old errors and drawbacks, to gain new knowledge, to learn new skills, to better oneself, and to strive for a brighter future day by day.

Newton said three centuries ago, "If I have seen further, it is by standing on the shoulders of giants." The accumulated knowledge and collected wisdom are the common property of human beings and, therefore, what Newton meant by the "giant's shoulders". To know what is intended for oneself is to better utilize the giants' shoulders and to abide by the moral legacy. To become a new person every day is to constantly strive for a better tomorrow. The above mentioned are the ideals of Tomorrow Studio and the guidelines for our publications. We welcome people who share our ideals and our dreams to come join us and help create a brighter tomorrow.

Acknowledgments

I would like to dedicate this book to the late Mr. Sheu Yuan-dong, former Governor of the Central Bank of China and a great teacher and friend. He devoted his entire life to the development of Taiwan's banking sector, even to his very last breath. In the second half of 1997, using great skill and wisdom, he guided Taiwan's banking system through the worst part of the East Asian financial crisis. On February 16, 1998, on his return to Taiwan from a conference in Indonesia, he perished in the CAL plane crash of that date. He was 71. The death of Governor Sheu is a great loss for Taiwan, and a terrible personal tragedy for me. On that day, it was as if on my tired heart a new wound had opened.

I wish to express gratitude to Mr. Jonathan Ross, President of ABN AMRO Asia Securities, Taiwan for translating You Too Can Understand --- The East Asian Financial Crisis. *His extensive knowledge, vast experience, and fluent writing style have rendered the book in a splendid and impressive translation in English.*

My thanks are also due to Ms. T. Miriam Chung for translating Mr. C. C. Tsai's comics and for proofreading the translation of C. C. Tsai's "The World of Fate".

Foreword
Observing the Minute Details
By Dr. P.K. Chiang

(Chairman of the Council for Economic Planning and
Development of the Executive Yuan of the Republic of China.)

From July 1997 to the present the nations of Asia have been mired in the East Asian Financial Crisis and have faced challenges of a severity seldom seen before. Owing to Taiwan's strong economic fundamentals, sound industrial base, low levels of external debt, cumulative current account surpluses, and large foreign currency reserves, Taiwan has luckily been spared the brunt of the turmoil. From this point onwards, the government should continue to seek to stabilize Taiwan's financial markets, speed reconstruction of the public sector administrative system, and strengthen Taiwan's economy.

We must always make use of all available resources to surmount the problems that confront us. The researches on the East Asian Financial Crisis provided by the many domestic think tanks have been of great value in promoting the stable development of the Taiwan economy. In this respect, I am particularly gratified to see published this work by Mr. Sayling

Wen, Vice Chairman of Inventec Group. Mr. Wen's first-hand insights into the Asian Crisis throw new light on the subject and are of special value given his position as a leader in the business community. His careful analysis of the subject matter, important suggestions as to how to repair the damage caused by the crisis, and advice on how to avoid future crises are all extremely welcome and make highly worthwhile reading for all, especially for those in Taiwan's many small- and medium- sized businesses.

Mr. Wen not only provides his own philosophy concerning how to successfully run a business, he also follows up his observations with concrete advice. The contents address issues relevant to both businessmen and government leaders, and the work offers a framework through which business and government leaders can fruitfully exchange ideas. At the same time, the work opens the way for the business community to become even more involved in the arena of public policy, and this book should be of especially great importance as the government seeks to formulate ways to enhance the competitiveness of Taiwanese industry. For this reason I am particularly glad to have the opportunity to provide this foreword.

Foreword
Historical Inevitability
Dr. Casper Shih

（Chairman of the Global Chinese Competitiveness Foundation）

While most corporations have just decided to begin investing in foreign production bases, Inventec has already extended its corporate boarders to include Malaysia, China, as well as other countries. The key individual who has brought Inventec into the international realm is the author of this book, Mr. Sayling Wen, group vice chairman of Inventec Group. He is an entrepreneur who not only possesses vision is his business, but also has experienced success in technological R&D and corporate management. Along with his specialty in international finance and trade, his various experiences in international management are the key factor for his success in writing this book and providing keen and accurate analysis and solution to the East Asian financial crisis.

Since the outbreak of the East Asian financial crisis, there have been many reports by various media on the conditions of the different countries in this region. Many experts and scholars have even gone further, attempting to find the reasons that have caused this upheaval. So far, they have managed to formulate their own action plans and strategies for a solution. Taiwan, despite having only been affected in a limited and contained manner, is also a focus for various discussions. In this book, the author attempts to go in-depth to figure-out all the cause-and-effect relationships regarding this issue. The key to the problem in East Asian countries is that they all adopt economic development policies that emphasize exports therefore causing disruptions to the production-sales equilibrium while at the same time creating excess supply. Simply speaking, it is an issue of competitiveness.

In reality, to lead a country's economic development forward is like riding a bicycle. If you don't continue peddling forward, you won't be able to maintain balance (equilibrium) and you will fall. The East Asian financial crisis that began last July came without early warning and is an excellent real-life example.

In the past, the only competitive advantage that Asian-Pacific countries had over other developing countries was cheap land and labor. In response to the vast market demands of the United States and Europe, every country has taken an export-oriented approach. Even though there are numerous foreign corporations that have invested in production bases, they have mostly imported already constructed components and parts, and the only part of the process done in these bases is the final assembly. When the market supply exceeds demand, this type of industrial framework has no substantial foundation and will therefore face severe challenges and risk elimination. In addition to this, the dependence on political maneuvers to control financial operations and limit finance liberalization prohibits a country's healthy and normal operations. It can also cause direct and negative impacts on the whole economic development of a country.

The author further points out that when the U.S., Japan and other advanced countries were brought into the region, the seed for financial crisis was planted. East Asian countries then began mishandling and misusing vast amounts of this new capital without knowing how to use it to their best advantage. In another words, for these Asian countries to move beyond the current financial situation, they needed to develop their own core competence, strengthen their economic base, and rebuild corporate confidence. Otherwise these East Asian countries would have no choice but suffer more cruel blows from the dynamic global financial environment.

Many people feel that financial-economic business is an extremely difficult issue and should be left only to professionals. To the contrary, it is actually something that all of us should take up and make part of our common knowledge. Daily life, whether it includes purchasing and sales, managing assets, or investments, the more we understand the changes in the global financial environment, the easier it is for us to learn how to manage our own "monetary future." In this book, the author takes on a corporate perspective and describes the causes and effects of the situation in easy-to-understand detail. In addition, he also discusses the possible and feasible solutions to the problems. Through the author's description, the readers can clearly and in-depth understand the current situation of each East Asian countries. The author's quantified analysis can also enhance the reader's grasp of the international market place. In terms of developing a long-term strategy to deal with the environment, the author's concepts, such as building an independent wealth-creating system and developing/utilizing computer and communication systems, are not only unique but also visionary, and are something that shouldn't be missed.

I would like to use this opportunity to commend the author. His experiences and concepts are special and unique. At the same time, I truly believe that the East Asian economic crisis is not something incidental. Like the author says, it is a historical inevitability that is a part of humanity's cultural transformation. As long as the necessary conditions are met, it will eventually occur again. It is my hope that individuals and corporations will have the opportunity to absorb the wisdom of this book and become winners in the extremely competitive world of the future.

Contents

Preface

Imagine a worker living in one of Jakarta's suburbs. He works long and hard each day, and with the sweat of his brow may be able to earn 10,000 Rupiah per day. He saves his money and every three or four months goes to Jakarta to do some sightseeing, to eat out, and to buy basic necessities. On one particular day, he wears his best clothes, brings his hard-earned money, and goes to his favourite market to buy the items he needs. Suddenly, he discovers that the things he wants to buy have risen in price by several-fold. In the space of a few short months, the Rupiah has fallen from 2,500 against the US dollar to as low as 12,000 against the greenback. In the past, he had earned over US$4 per day, but now he earns the equivalent of only around US$0.80 per day. The items he wants to buy are mainly imported, and prices are linked to the US dollar. Therefore, when converted to Rupiah, they are now several times more expensive. The worker of whom we speak doesn't understand the intricacies of international finance. In anger, he picks up a stone and smashes the shop window. The worker is not alone in his anger and frustration, and soon hundreds of others in similar circumstances join in looting the shop until finally the police arrive to restore calm.

Over the past half year, similar events have occurred in Indonesia on countless occasions. Such events reflect not only frustration at the erosion of the purchasing powers of the Rupiah, but also a sense of deep disappointment in traditional values. A worker, who works hard all his life, even though he himself has nothing to do with the currency or stock markets, suddenly finds that he has lost a good portion of his personal wealth.

In Taiwan, a recent college graduate prepares to go abroad to study. He works as a teaching assistant in university during the day. At night he works as a tutor. His goal is to save US$20,000 over a two year period（NT$540,000）. Just when he is about to reach his goal, the NT dollar slides over 25% to around 34:1 against the US dollar. Suddenly, he finds he needs to save not NT$540,000 but rather NT$680,000. He has to save an additional NT$140,000 if he is to meet his goal. In other words, he must work for an additional half-year, and hence he must delay his study plans by a full year. Youth is precious. How many years can he afford to give up? When asked how he feels, he replies helplessly "Never in a million years did I imagine that such a disaster could occur."

Both of the foregoing stories are instructive in the sense that they highlight the scope of the East Asian Financial Crisis. Indeed, under the relentless battering of the Asian financial storm, whether one was in Indonesia (the region hit hardest by the storm) or in Taiwan (the region least hurt in the turmoil) one couldn't escape the damage caused by the crisis. Governments, businesses, or banks: all were hurt badly in the chaos, as were rich and poor alike.

Indeed the financial destruction that resulted from the crisis as of the end of 1997 may have surpassed the financial destruction sustained throughout all of World War II. Throughout history, war has often been waged to occupy territory and subjugate foreign peoples, with the ultimate aim of taking wealth from the vanquished. In today's world, the East Asian Financial Crisis has taught us that just by connecting to a computer network and entering a few keystrokes into a computer, a speculator can also take vast sums of wealth from the vanquished. Without sending a single soldier into battle, the speculator can thus wage a full-scale war of conquest.

How did such a situation come about? How will the crisis unfold going forward? How should we prepare ourselves for the future? These questions are not just for the experts to answer. It behooves all of us to better understand these issues. For no matter where we are, a financial crisis similar to the current one can attack us and steal our wealth at any time.

This book *You Too Can Understand - The East Asian Financial Crisis* is written for all to understand. The book contains no technical language or statistics or charts. The language is simple and easy to understand, and explains the causes, effects, and proper policy response associated with the East Asian Financial Crisis.

When I first started to write this book, I came quickly to learn that the East Asian Financial Crisis was an extremely complex issue. To describe such a complex issue using easily understandable language was not a simple task. I read many treatises on the subject written by experts in the field, and conducted interviews with many of those experts as well. In mid-January 1998, I was fortunate to participate in a trade delegation led by Council for Economic Planning and Development Chairman Dr. P. K. Chiang. Our group visited the nations of Southeast Asia, and included Cabinet-level officials, senior bankers, industry association officials, and leading Taiwanese businessmen accompanied by a cohort of journalists. Altogether there were 70 or 80 group members. We met with senior government and business leaders in all the major Southeast Asian countries and exchanged ideas. This trip in particular strengthened my impressions regarding the nature of the East Asian Financial Crisis.

Under the tutelage of a number of economic experts, I finally managed to complete this book and was particularly honoured that CEPD Chairman Dr. P. K. Chiang agreed to write the foreword on my behalf. After spending a week traveling with Dr. Chiang throughout Southeast Asia, I developed a keen appreciation for his tireless efforts on behalf of Taiwanese industry. I was also particularly impressed with his very straightforward and logical way of thinking and approach to problems, as well as his articulateness and personal warmth. My week with Dr. Chiang also brought me to the realization that Taiwan's economic miracle was made possible not only by the hard work of Taiwan's businessmen and workers, but also by the assiduous efforts and careful planning of the island's government officials.

We hope that the current crisis has reached a climax, but just as the book describes, financial crises seem to have about them a certain historical inevitability. If the wrong conditions emerge again in the future, then just as a low pressure front in the Pacific has the potential to evolve into a Typhoon, so might another financial crisis strike again. The financial damage which a financial crisis can cause is on a par with the damage caused by war or natural disaster. In the future, the amount of resources a nation devotes to preventing a potential financial crisis should be on a par with the amount of resources spent on national defense. Each citizen, furthermore, should be familiar with the issues surrounding a financial crisis, for in the future, such a crisis can strike at any time and sap our hard-earned wealth.

At this point, I would especially like to thank Singapore's Ambassador at large, Mr. Nathan, and international financial expert, Mr. Jonathan Ross (President of ABN AMRO Asia Securities, Taiwan), leading Taiwan financial authority Mr. Springfield Lai (Head of Price Waterhouse, Taiwan), Asian strategy and management authority Dr. Casper Shih (former President of China Productivity Center), Vice President of the Export-Import Bank of The Republic of China, Ms. S. Y. Chen (former Director of the Monetary Bureau of the R.O.C. Ministry of Finance), and leading Taiwanese financial authority, Mr. H. S. Wang. All of these individuals contributed greatly to this book and in doing so have expressed deep sympathy and concern for all the people of Asia and indeed the world over who have suffered as a result of the East Asian Financial Crisis.

Prelude

The most significant event of the decade for most Asian nations has been the financial crisis, which has swept the Asian region since mid-1997. Governments, businesses, and individuals, in the blink of an eye, found themselves trapped in a storm of unprecedented proportions. The financial disaster which has befallen the region struck without warning, and left nearly all in its path virtually powerless to react. The term "Financial Storm" in no way falls short in measuring the chaos caused by this terrible event.

In analysing the devastation, it is pertinent to pose a number of questions. How was it that the financial storm clouds gathered in the first place? How long will the financial maelstrom continue to affect the region? What impact will the crisis have on the region in the years ahead? Finally and most importantly, what can be done in response

to the damage caused by the crisis? These questions form the focus of discussion in this book.

1.   East Asian Financial Crisis: Causes

When there were problems such as an imbalance in supply and demand, an over-investment in conventional consumption-related industries and an over-reliance on foreign investment East Asian countries quickly become the attack targets of foreign exchange investors and speculators.

According to some of the world's most renowned economists, there are nine principal causes for the financial woes in the region. These are as follows:

Largo

1.1　Imbalance in Supply and Demand

I'll never forget a visit I once took to Ireland, a clean and beautiful country. The Irish Industrial Development Authority had invited me to inspect plant sites in Ireland and so we drove to several locations across the island. I visited one industrial park after another and was deeply impressed to see how modern and well planned each one was. One stood out in particular. We stopped in front of a factory in that industrial park. The factory was unoccupied, but boasted a complete set of all the latest in lighting, air-conditioning, and power equipment, and was also set against a stunning natural setting. All around were fields of emerald green nestled against a backdrop of majestic mountains. From inside the factory, we looked out on the enormous parking lot outside, the parking lot bigger even than the factory itself. Even the dining hall appeared as if it belonged in a five-star hotel. When I asked how much the factory cost, the Authority executive answered "two and a half million dollars".

"Two and a half million dollars?" I asked him, trying to hide my incredulity. I knew that such a factory in Taiwan would cost at least US$10m.

"That's right. We spent fifteen million dollars to build it, but there are no products to produce here, so we're looking to get it off our hands as fast as possible. There are many other plants across Europe in the same boat as this one."

For someone accustomed to East Asia, it is difficult to imagine just how low asset values are in other parts of the world. In particular, Asians tend to see factories as symbols of growth. A factory is used to produce products, which are then sold to earn money. Many have viewed this chain as unbreakable: almost a law of nature. Many Asians even view factories as important architectural landmarks.

After returning from Ireland, I took away a heightened appreciation for the idea that production must always have its roots in market demand. If the goods it produces are not marketable, even the most modern factory is nothing more than a television set without programming. It is, in other words, useless.

We now examine the relevance of this example in the context of the current economic crisis. Since the 1960s, East Asian countries, led by Japan and the four tiger economies - Hong Kong, Korea, Singapore and

Taiwan - with a combined population of under 200 million, have supplied manufactured merchandise of all kinds to the developed countries of North America and Western Europe, with a combined population of 600m. This simple equation had led to the rapid economic rise of the five countries over the thirty year period beginning in 1960.

During this time, owing to civil war, internal conflicts or ideological considerations, most other countries in the region did not engage in export-oriented production to the same extent. The start of the current decade ushered in a new era of peace throughout the region, however, and leaders in those "laggard" countries began to realize that the best way to improve the lot of their citizens was through export-led economic development. At the same time, Japan and the four tiger countries sought to move production to new and cheaper locations as rising wage costs at home eroded manufacturing competitiveness. As a result, many new production plants were established throughout East Asia and the region's 2 billion people prepared themselves for an expected economic upturn.

Unfortunately, markets in North America and

Europe did not expand to the extent expected and this resulted in supply heavily outweighing demand. Suppliers with the highest costs or weakest competitive positions were the first to feel the effects. A Thai production-line worker, for instance, doing the same job as his counter-part in China but at double the cost was bound to suffer. To state the matter starkly, it was from this imbalance that the economic crisis erupted.

1.2   Over-investment in Conventional Consumption-related Industries

One day, I went to visit a friend in Shanghai. His company had recently moved to a brand-new office building. After I entered his luxurious private office, he opened a pair of Venetian blinds to look out on the Shanghai sunset. I could see high-rise office towers and condominiums in all directions, as well as worksites with cranes and bulldozers as far as the eye could see. Directly below I spotted the ring expressway which encircles the downtown district. In the fading light of day, the expressway snaked like a river through fields of blinking neon lights and throngs of people moving to and fro down below.

"Look at that," my friend said. "What you see is the spirit of Shanghai, and Shanghai's speed in building is just like the old saying goes: 'a style a year, a revolution in three years." Pointing off in the distance to a subway station, he continued. "Look over there. Above the station is a department store, and next to it are a restaurant and a dance hall complex. Nearby is a bowling alley, not to mention new office towers and high-end condominiums. Five or six years ago, that spot was just a bunch of low-rise housing and empty lots. The pace of development here is unbelievable."

Thinking back to five or six years prior, to the time I first arrived in Shanghai, it was undeniable that the city had changed completely. In the intervening years, I came to appreciate the efficiency of the Shanghainese and the Shanghai "spirit" of which my friend spoke. But I was also filled with a sense of unease. Looking at my friend I smiled and said, "construction eats up money. What Shanghai really needs now is to build a system that earns money for the city."

On hearing this, my friend froze for a second, as if

he had just been splashed with cold water, then admitted grudgingly, "I suppose you do have a point".

Flooded with foreign investment during the boom years of the 1980s and early 1990s, many countries in East Asia simply did not have the requisite experience in spending such a vast amount of money prudently. In an effort to improve living standards, players in the region invested huge amounts of money in department stores, supermarkets, fast food chains, discotheques, bowling alleys, KTVs, office buildings, skyscrapers and highways. However, without a solid foundation for wealth creation, these investments were destined to fail.

Previously, economists classified economic systems into primary industries, such as agriculture or mining, secondary industries such as manufacturing, and tertiary industries such as services. This classification is based on job category. As society has evolved and professions have become increasingly diverse, this classification plainly is no longer suitable as it fails to cover the entire range of economic activities. As an example, the above system does not account adequately for a person who stays at home play the stock market. Today, economic activity is more effectively classified into a different set of three sectors:

1.2a   Wealth Creation

Wealth- creating activities are those economic activities that create value by using resources effectively or which create the same value by using fewer resources. Our forefathers once had to live as nomads, following the grass and waters. Only later was the planting of crops discovered. This led in turn to agricultural development, which permitted the establishment of permanent settlements built with gravel and cement. After the industrial revolution, mankind discovered how to make best use of a wide variety of natural resources, including petroleum products, electricity and others. These discoveries then helped to improve the quality of life for all. In the past ten years, mankind has further learned to fully utilize computers - one of our most precious resources - and in line with this development, human intelligence and creativity have become key resources for the creation of value or wealth. Sand is transformed into silicon, silicon is then transformed into integrated circuits (ICs), IC's are used to make computers and microcontrollers, which in turn control motor vehicles and aircraft. This type of process - the process of using natural resources and human intelligence to create value - is what we mean by developing systems that create value or wealth.

Another type of system for wealth creation has to do with those systems that conserve natural resources and thus arrive at the same effect as those that create value directly. Genetic improvement of crops which allows less fertilizer to produce the same amount of crops, or equipment which uses half the power to produce the same results all qualify as value creating systems that achieve results by conserving resources. Systems that create value are those systems that use resources in the most efficient manner to create wealth or which reduce the amount of resources needed to create a given amount of value.

1.2b   Trading —A Zero-Sum Game

The second type of economic activity is trade, or activities that allocate capital and goods more effectively. In the West, this type of activity is referred to as a Zero-Sum Game. It should be emphasised that this type of activity does not create value. If Mr. Kowalski buys a house for $1,000,000 and sells the house to Mr. Washington for $1,100,000, and then Mr. Washington sells the house to Mr. Califano for $1,200,000, the result is that Messrs. Kowalski and Washington each made $100,000 and Mr. Califano gets the house he wanted. The house, nevertheless, has not changed in any fundamental respect. It has not acquired any new attributes of value. Economists refer to such an economic system as a "trading system".

As collection and dissemination of information becomes more advanced, trading activities have undergone constant change and many predict that after the Internet achieves global penetration, the volume of inter-personal trade will increase dramatically. The stock market is the most representative trading activity. Regardless of whether the stock market rises or falls, and regardless of how many people make or lose money in the market, no value is created (or lost) in the market's fluctuations. In this sense, stock trading is a Zero-Sum game, for the amount of money won in the market is almost exactly identical to the amount of money lost in the market. Yet, despite the fact that trading activity does not create value, it can promote the allocation of capital to its most efficient uses.

1.2c   Consumption

The third classification of economic activity is that of consumption. When one buys a bed in a department store, or decides to install an air-conditioning system in one's house, or eats a meal in a restaurant, all of these activities improve the quality of one's life and are consumption activities. The economic system that provides these activities is referred to as the consumption system. Such a system utilizes wealth in pursuit of improving the quality of life.

In any country, there are those who build homes (participants in the wealth creation system), those who broker properties (participants in the trading system), and those who purchase homes (participants in the consumption system). If actors in an economy are spread evenly across the three systems, then the economy is likely to develop in a healthy, balanced fashion. However, if the building of homes is left to foreigners, and local participants are limited to the trading or purchase of homes, then such an economy is likely to face serious obstacles as it seeks to develop.

At present, the wealth-creating activities of many developing countries are in the hands of foreign investors as investors in many developing countries have placed their own capital into the consumption sector. Many of these consumption activities or services are becoming obsolete in developed countries. Over-investment in such activities takes up valuable foreign currency reserves and increases foreign debt significantly. A focus on consumption-related investment also helped to precipitate the recent crisis.

1.3   Over-reliance on Foreign Investment and Failure to Develop Systems for Wealth Creation

What happens to a poor family living a quiet life when a rich relative moves in and offers to help with house repairs, mending of the carpet, and installation of an air-conditioning system or other appliances? What if the rich relative also buys a car for his poorer cousins? The poor family's standard of living rises quickly. As the poor family becomes accustomed to a higher standard of living, it would not be surprising if began to borrow to pay for new clothes and other expensive items. When friends or neighbors see such luxurious items in their "newly rich" neighbour's house, they certainly would be happy to lend, for would not the suddenly well-off family have the wherewithal to repay any loans extended? The suddenly well-off family now finds its living expenses rising by the day, yet its income has not risen at all. Meanwhile, debt piles onto debt. One day, the rich relative leaves, and the suddenly "well-off" family not only returns to poverty, but also finds itself crushed under a mountain of debt.

This is not simply a metaphor: any nation, which is too reliant on foreign capital (especially short-term foreign capital), is bound to meet the same fate as the poor family in our example. Recently, many countries in East Asia aside from Japan and the four tiger countries have relied on foreign direct investment to fuel economic growth. These countries not only have suffered to a varying extent from over-investment in relatively unproductive sectors, the capital markets in these countries are also over-exposed to short-term foreign portfolio funds. These funds tend to rush in and out of a country, not only creating an illusion of prosperity, but sometimes also destroying traditional social values. More importantly, without adequate wealth-creating systems of their own, these countries can merely look on as foreign investors take advantage of the host country's cheap labour and natural resources. Often, the host country is unable to fully benefit from the know-how and experience brought in by foreign direct investors and is thus unable to establish its own wealth-creating systems.

1.4   Failure of Large Corporations to Restructure

In the past two decades, large companies in North America and Europe have radically restructured their operations to cater to the demands of modern society. Privatisation of state-owned companies, massive lay-offs and the promotion of early retirement have become commonplace on both continents but remain for the large part anathema to countries in East Asia. Many state-owned enterprises in East Asia as well as large private companies in Japan and Korea (often larger than their counterparts in North America and

Europe) have consistently failed to implement profound organizational restructuring.

East Asia's population of two billion can be divided into three main blocks. The first block, with a combined population of nearly 200m, consists of Japan and Korea, where the problem to date has been that large companies have yielded to the pressures of society, culture and personal relationships and have failed to restructure. Greater China, encompassing Mainland China, Hong Kong and Taiwan, includes a combined total population of 1.3bn and has been less-severely affected because corporations in the region tend to be highly flexible and cost-effective producers. At some point, however, restructuring of China's state-owned enterprises may shake economic and financial stability in the region. Lastly, the 500 million people of Southeast Asia face the danger of being left behind China in terms of both cost competitiveness and industrial sophistication.

The developed economies of North America and Europe came to grips with the changing competitive pattern long ago and began restructuring their industries accordingly. Unfortunately, the same did not occur in East Asia where policy makers ignored the danger signals, and thereby allowed the seeds of economic crisis to take root.

1.5   Creation of a Bubble Economy

"Bubble Economy" is a term heard often of late, but what does the term actually signify? If one pour beer or cola into a glass, the top layers consists of bubbles or froth. If one pours too quickly, the froth may even spill over the sides of the glass. If one waits a moment, however, the bubbles gradually disappear, and one suddenly discovers that the glass is only partially full. The initial appearance of fullness was only illusory. This, then, is the origin of the term "bubble economy".

Imagine a street with 50 similar houses each housing one family, and imagine that each house is worth $2 million. One day, a house on the street sells for $10 million. Suddenly, the other 49 residents on the street think that they are $8 million wealthier. Some might mortgage their house, perhaps for $3 million. Those that borrow on their homes might go out to spend their money, thus helping to pick up business in the neighborhood.

Economic prosperity is typically built as those that create wealth then become consumers. In the preceding example, however, economic prosperity is built on the illusion of wealth creation, translated into borrowing, and finally to consumption. What happens if one day the housing price in our example dropped back down to $2 million? What happens when those that mortgaged their homes are unable to repay their loans? Such problems are typical of "bubble economies".

The most obvious example of a "bubble economy" can be seen in the stock market. When stock market prices suddenly rise sharply, those holding stock all feel wealthy. Some begin to spend more money, and thus the illusion of wealth creation takes root. This is what we mean by "bubble economy".

How was it that the bubble economies developed throughout Southeast Asia? The earliest foreign investments in the region were involved in Foreign Direct Investment (FDI). Over the past ten years, especially following the end of the Cold War period, the political situation in Southeast Asia gradually stabilized and the region's supply of low-cost labour, combined with high savings and large potential markets attracted large volumes of investment from Europe, the US, Japan, and the Dragon economies. Such volumes of foreign investment sped economic development in the region, and helped to boost economic growth rates in the region to levels well above the world average.

FDI was followed by waves of short-term capital

Rapid economic growth in the Southeast Asian nations helped to promote infrastructure investment, as well as growth in the region's stock and property markets, and this growth in turn helped to attract short-term foreign capital into the region.

Foreign Debt Increased

Given massive foreign direct and portfolio investment in the region, which came in addition to the region's high saving rate, it would appear to the casual observer that there should have been no need for Asian countries to borrow heavily, yet borrow they did. Why did they borrow? One reason common throughout the region was to borrow to take advantage of the regions stable currency regime. A "stable currency regime" essentially means that the region's currency move in tandem with the US dollar and only fluctuates in a narrow range relative to the US currency. In the case of Hong Kong, the range was around HKD7.7: USD1, and in Taiwan the rate settled around 27. The benefit of maintaining a stable currency regime is that such a regime makes for easier financial management, especially as the US dollar is the most international currency available.

What did the linkage to the US dollar mean for the rest of Asia? The US dollar exchange rate fluctuates daily, and the US commands not only the greatest accumulation of wealth in the world, but also has the greatest number of financial experts in the world. These experts devote themselves to identifying the most suitable exchange rate for the US dollar against other world currencies. Most East Asian countries rely on US-dollar-based external trade as a means of accumulating wealth. Such a peg to the US-dollar makes sense as it allows such countries to more easily keep track of costs and avoid manipulation of the currency. The drawback to maintaining a peg, however, is that demand for the US dollar is not always aligned with demand for the local currency. Inflation rates across the region and in the US also differ. Demand for a particular currency will affect the interest rate in that currency. When demand for a particular currency increases, in theory interest rates for that currency should rise.

Owing to rapid growth in the East Asian economies, demand for the region's domestic currencies tended to be high. Interest rates in the region thus tended to be higher than those in the US. As a result, many corporations in the region began to borrow US dollars at relatively lower interest rates, and then converted such borrowings into local currency deposits, thus earning the interest spread. As foreign banks and financial institutions were generally bullish on the East Asian economy, they were willing to extend large amounts of loans to companies in the region. As direct investors, portfolio investors, and speculators seeking to win big on interest spreads flowed into the region, the property market and stock markets began to froth. After tremendous gains in equities and properties became headline news, these gains attracted still more foreign capital into the region, thus compounding the effect of the bubble economy.

1.6 Problems in Oversight of the Banking and Financial Sectors

For those who grew up in the West, it is sometimes difficult to appreciate the significance of "The Bank" in Asian culture. In Asia, banks generally occupy the best locations in the city, and boast imposing architecture enhanced by luxurious interiors. To work in a bank is to be given a "Golden Rice Bowl" along with accompanying privileges and status in society. When entering a bank, the average citizen is likely to feel the same sort of inner inadequacy as his ancestors might have when entering a palace, and even the act of withdrawing one's own money from one's own bank account might fill one with a sense of accomplishment or pride.

In the eyes of many Asian citizens, the nation's banks are seen as organs of the government. The financial sector in many Asian countries carries with it a heavy burden of responsibility to the nation, and is often shrouded in a sort of mystique. Care of the financial sector is typically placed in the hands of a small number of highly-trusted officials. This is similar to the situation in many companies, where the accounting function is entrusted to the CEO's closest confidantes. Drawing further on the analogy to the corporate sector, however, we note the increasing trend whereby large or public corporations in the interest of maintaining their shareprice must open up their accounts to provide a degree of transparency acceptable to investors.

Despite trends toward greater openness, the financial management practices seen in the public sector in many East Asian countries remain behind-the-times. Indeed, it seems to the casual observer that many senior public officials in the financial sector have become even more conservative with age.

A nation's financial system is at once a complex and powerful organism. Over past decades, however, the financial system in the typical East Asian country has been overseen by a small number of officials and experts who have not had the need to make public critical financial information. Only a select few had need of important national financial information, and therefore, the inner workings of the system and possible problems or areas of weakness remained hidden. As the backlog of problems had grown by the year, long buried problems began to surface after the

East Asian Financial Crisis broke, and the emergence of these once-hidden problems caused the crisis to grow rapidly in proportion and scope.

1.7   Liberalization and Internationalization of the Financial Markets

Financial liberalization and internationalization have become inescapable trends in the current age. Fostered by rapid changes in information technology, booming international trade and the advent of the information age have led to the creation of the 'Global Village'. Nations that aspire to develop cannot afford to be left outside of the global financial and information network as domestic markets open up and globalization becomes increasingly inevitable. Most important is that when a country or region liberalizes its financial markets, supporting software infrastructure such as an effective legal system and regulatory environment becomes crucial in determining the success or failure of the liberalization initiative. A highway is a wonderful thing but can be very dangerous if bicycles are allowed to use it.

With the majority of the world's financial markets

already liberalized, international investors and speculators now treat the currency of a given country as an indicator for that nation's economic prospects. As a result, the Forex market has become the largest financial market in the world. In days past, individuals with no dealings in financial commodities remained largely unaffected by capital market turbulence. At present, however, currency fluctuations can sometimes be more violent than those in the stock market, and none is immune to the consequences that arise when enormous international investment funds move across borders at high speed on enhanced computer and communications networks. East Asian countries are faced with a further dilemma of not only of having to open up their financial markets, but also of having to work within the framework of traditional value systems resistant to change in the infrastructural software. This analogy is similar to trying to drive a jalopy on the autobahn, and the result can be dangerous.

1.8   Failure to Keep up with Advancing Financial Technology

An American financial expert once sat beside me

on an airplane. On learning that I was a notebook PC manufacturer, he proclaimed to me that his notebook PC was the best product that he had ever bought in his entire life. He related to me how it previously took a very large computer system to analyse a country's economic and financial situation and how today, it can all be done with a simple notebook PC. The wider use of computer and telecommunications equipment over the past twenty years has raised the importance of information technology to unprecedented levels and this has critical implications for financial services. The financial executive that still makes decisions relying on telephones, meetings and paper reports has no idea of how inferior he is to the financial expert equipped with a notebook PC and cellular phone. I picture this as equivalent to an ancient warrior armed with a bow and arrow looking down from his horse at a man in a business suit holding a small pistol, and not realising that the tiny pistol can kill him in an instant. One by-word that we never want to forget in these times is that "the field of business, is like the field of battle".

1.9   An Historical Inevitability

The information age represents not simply a hope for the future but is an era that has already dawned. The wide use of technology has resulted in global financial networks that comprise the first wave of the new age.

In this information era, only those companies that are abreast of technological developments can hope to remain competitive in the global marketplace. The problems of supply/demand imbalance, over-reliance on foreign investment, lack of a wealth-creating system, over-investment in the wrong areas and lack of restructuring in East Asia were all identified very quickly by financial analysts once markets were liberalized. Countries with gaping structural deficiencies then became the easy prey of Forex investors and speculators.

Clearly, the recent financial crisis in East Asia was not simply an accident or a freak occurrence. Just as the industrial revolution fundamentally changed the world some two hundred years ago, so too has the information revolution brought about enormous change in the midst of the current regional upheaval. Those able to foresee the implications of the coming change stand to benefit most.

The key question regarding the crisis lies not in when it will end, but how it can be prevented from happening again. Other relevant questions which demand answers include how a country can best position its currency in the context of the vast global financial network, how it can guard its currency from attack, and how it can use the available technologies and manpower resources to run an efficient financial system. These matters are of the utmost importance - on a par with issues of national defense - and should be monitored daily as the highest priority by those responsible for economic policy.

Interlude

Right after the East Asian financial crisis, an honest and decent person asked fate,

I don't gamble, and I don't speculate. How come the money in my pocket is only worth half of what it used to be?

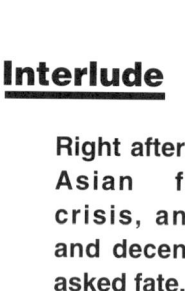

Today, in the end of the century, the rules of the money game have changed. Although you don't gamble, your money has long been used to gamble by other people.

hahaha

hahaha

hahaha

But I keep the money safe in my pocket. Nobody has stolen it and gambled with it.

They don't need to use the money in your pocket. What they use is their currency of the same value as the money in your pocket. If they win, they make a big profit and the money in your pocket depreciates.

2.　How the Crisis Occurred

There is no national boundary when it comes to money. By simply connecting to a computer network and entering a few keystrokes into a computer, speculators can destroy the financial system of a country with absolutely no need to deploy troops.

Next, we will examine the specifics of what exactly happened in East Asia to cause the recent turmoil.

Theme Melody

When international financial investors and speculators spotted weak points in the financial systems of East Asian countries, they typically proceeded in a number of ways.

2.1 Borrow Local Currency

Speculators or other financial investors borrow local currency using foreign assets or credit as a guarantee. There are various techniques and variations which may be employed.

2.2 Siphon off Foreign Currency Reserves

All countries have some degree of foreign currency reserves and foreign debt. Usually, local currency is used in domestic transactions and foreign currencies are used in international transactions. After borrowing local currency, the speculator then proceeds to buy up foreign currency in the host country, rendering the host country short of foreign currency reserves and unable to pay its foreign debts.

2.3   Drive Down the Exchange Rate

In order to buy back foreign currency, the host country has to sell the local currency. This typically leads to a devaluation of the local currency. Meanwhile, worried about further devaluation of the local currency, local companies and individuals alike join the rush to buy foreign currency. The more people that do so, the faster the local currency devalues. This can lead to panic with the net result being that the local currency plummets. It was a vicious circle. The dramatic depreciation of local currency downgraded the international credit rating for the host country, and made it more difficult to borrow foreign funds to stabilize the value of the local currency.

2.4   "Borrow a lot, Repay a little"

When the host country's currency reaches a bottom, the speculator buys local currency at a very cheap rate to pay back the original loan in the host country's currency. By borrowing at a high value and returning at a low value, the speculator makes a sizeable profit. In history, people would have had trouble imagining the possibility of: "Stealing a nation's wealth, without using a single soldier or troop, or even setting foot on that nation's soil."

Most experts believe the losses East Asian countries registered in the current crisis easily exceed US$100bn, far higher that the financial losses incurred even in World War II. It has been fashionable of late in some circles to ask even whether the recent financial crisis occurred as the result of a plot by Western nations. Personally, I feel that the likelihood that such a plot existed is extremely small. In particular, the main winners as a result of the recent turmoil are not nations, but individuals, corporations, and speculators. In addition, the roots of the problem run deep and grew steadily over time. The problems that emerged in July 1997 were merely the result of speculators and investors spotting an opportunity to make money.

Most important now is how we address the problems that have emerged in connection with the crisis. Up to now, responsibility for the losses and the actual losses resulting from the financial crisis have mainly been laid on the doorstep of the states involved and the IMF (International Monetary Fund). Many now advocate that responsibility should ultimately be pushed down to those that borrowed and lent funds to fuel the crisis. Some indeed advocate rewriting the rules governing the global financial system.

3. The Impact of the East Asia Financial Crisis

Don't think that the financial crisis is none of our business! Even if we don't buy stocks and don't do business, our wealth is also decreasing quietly.

Forte

3.1 Negative Effects

As a country's currency devalues dramatically and huge fortunes fall into the hands of international speculators, there are inevitably negative consequences for that country.

These include:

3.1a   Wealth reduction

Most countries in East Asia rely on international trade to import foreign products and services in order to improve living standards. Following the recent devaluations, imports are considerably more expensive in affected countries. Another way to view this is that citizens in the affected countries have experienced a corresponding fall in purchasing power.

3.1b   Loss of confidence in local currency

According to recent news reports, many people in Malaysia sold their houses and transferred the proceeds into foreign currency. Elsewhere, it was reported that the won devalued with such haste that even Korean school children changed their pocket money into foreign currencies. When the local currency plunges, confidence is shaken and households start to save in foreign currencies. In business, if a company bounces a cheque but remains in business, its suppliers are likely to say: "from now on payment in cash only, please." In East Asia now, some citizens even use foreign currencies for many domestic transactions, causing further declines in the local currency. When citizens lose confidence in their own currency, they are likely to say: "from now on, payment in hard currency only, please."

3.1c   Knock-on effects

In mid-January 1998, I visited Thailand and was struck by the remarkable improvement in Bangkok traffic. In the past, when I had visited Bangkok, the most difficult part of the experience was the Bangkok traffic jams. It is not uncommon for traffic to stand still for one or two hours, but on my recent visit, I encountered no traffic jams. When I asked the driver why the traffic in Bangkok had improved so considerably, he responded: "After the financial crisis, few can afford to buy cars or even gasoline. Banks have repossessed many cars, so altogether, there are many fewer cars on the roads." He then added: "In fact, the banks and auto dealerships have repossessed so many cars that they have no more room to store the cars."

When wealth in an economy is destroyed, one first typically witnesses a rapid conversion of the local currency into foreign currency. Reduction in purchasing power and insecurity about the future then typically forces consumers to cut back spending. Stock exchanges, real estate, car dealerships and department stores typically are the first to feel the effect. As businesses suffer, wages are cut and this in turn leads to a further reduction in consumption. The net effect is often a vicious cycle of falling wages and falling consumption which can even degenerate into a myriad of social problems including rising crime and even political instability.

3.1d Bankruptcies

Corporate bankruptcies typically rise sharply in connection with financial crises such as the current one. Apart from relying on internally generated capital, corporations also generally borrow from financial institutions, and rely on suppliers for working capital.

In addition, most corporations also provide working capital to their customers. As a result, a chain of debt links one corporation with another and with the banking system. When the East Asian financial crisis hit, many corporations with large foreign currency-denominated debt exposure faced immediate forex losses, and these companies were further unable in many cases to repay suppliers or lenders. Those companies, which were unable to recoup their loans in turn, were unable to repay loans to lenders or suppliers and thus a chain reaction erupted. Faced with mounting bad loans, banks were unable or unwilling to extend loans to potential corporate borrowers. This further exacerbated the financial difficulties of many corporations and led to the bankruptcies of many corporations and even banks.

Normally, when a corporation fails, it is because it has fallen victim to poor management or because it cannot cover its expenditures or because its book value becomes negative. When an economic chain reaction breaks the debt linkages that run throughout an economy, however, even healthy or well-run companies can fall victim. Many such companies may find themselves unable to raise working capital to process raw material into finished goods, or they may simply find that demand for their product has dried up, or that receivables have become uncollectable. While the book value of such companies may remain positive, the lack of working capital can still throw such companies into bankruptcy.

3.1e   Investment halted

When a financial crisis strikes, another problem area lies in faltering investment. New potential foreign investors generally suspend investments until worries of a further devaluation of the local currency dissipate. Domestic investment slows also owing to reduced domestic demand. Once capital stops flowing, depression sets in.

3.2   Positive Effects

The mirror has two faces, however, and there are some positive consequences of the recent crisis.

3.2a   Lower costs for exporters

The majority of international trade to and from

East Asia is settled in foreign currencies. As a result, the devaluation of local currencies means lower costs and improved competitiveness for Asian exporters. Some economists point out that this improved competitiveness may eventually hurt employment in other countries.

Of course, the boost to competitiveness that results from currency depreciation generally brings only short-term relief to a country. The "pleasure" derived from a currency devaluation may cause companies to slow plans to move up the value chain. The best response a corporation can make following a currency devaluation is to attempt to boost exports on the one hand, and at the same time seek aggressively to move up the value chain and thereby enhance corporate competitiveness.

The imbalance in regional supply and demand appears set to remain for some time to come. Reliance on low costs to promote exports thus is likely to only produce limited results in expanding profits. Only an emphasis on developing Core Competencies and a drive to enter into those business areas with the highest returns can produce significant or lasting profits. In addition, industries such as tourism are also worthwhile investments, both in terms of taking advantage of low costs that the region now offers and in terms of earning hard currencies.

3.2b   Self-examination

During the past decade, many countries in East Asia have grown at rates far in excess of world averages. This has led to overspending and consequently, a large number of unprofitable investments. The crisis, therefore, provides a sort of shock therapy for the region and affords it the opportunity for self-examination. In this sense, the recent turmoil may be a blessing in disguise for the region.

3.2c   Recognition of a Common East Asian Community

The Western media typically has termed the recent financial crisis the "Asian Financial Crisis". To be more correct, the crisis should be referred to as an "East Asian Financial Crisis". Indeed, the two billion strong area encompassing Japan, Korea, Greater China in the North, and ASEAN in the South has borne the brunt of the crisis, while other Asian regions have suffered much less dramatically from the turmoil at up to the present.

Though the nations of East Asia differ in much respect in terms of ethnicity, culture, language, and religion, history and geography have tied them together. In addition, economic similarities also bind them together. Economic dependence has already helped to create a sort of common East Asian Economic Community.

In the past ten years, intra-Asian investment, two-way trade, economic exchanges and tourism have boomed. In line with these developments, a new pan-Asian culture and lifestyle has also emerged. This new culture is reflected in everything from business language to satellite broadcasting to Karaoke, the latter having emanated from Tokyo to become a mainstream of night-time entertainment in Asian capitals as far away as Jakarta.

As the nations of East Asia share a common cultural heritage, they also tend to be more conservative at all levels of society, including in government. In this sense, they tend to stay clear of internal issues in neighboring countries. Thus we find that many regional organisations including the Asia

Pacific Economic Council (APEC), Pacific Economic Cooperation Council (PECC), and Pacific Basin Economic Council (PBEC), which address an Asian agenda, tend to be led by Western nations. In addition, in commercial affairs, many Asian countries tend to regard their neighbours as key economic competitors.

One positive development resulting from the East Asian Financial Crisis is the growing recognition that the nations of East Asia are locked into a common community. At the very least, this refers to a common economic community, as economic turbulence in one country in the region can easily spill over into other regional economies. Many scholars and exporters have warned that those countries which have escaped the brunt of the recent crisis must not take delight at the misery of their less fortunate neighbours, but rather should recognise that "we are all in the same boat together" and do everything possible to rescue those less fortunate neighbours. The current financial crisis should help the nations of East Asia to better understand each other, to discover common interests, and to work out the means of constructing a meaningful organisation to link the region's economies and financial systems.

Interlude

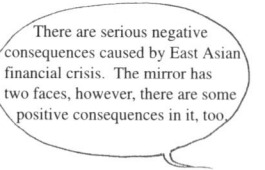

There are serious negative consequences caused by East Asian financial crisis. The mirror has two faces, however, there are some positive consequences in it, too.

What good does it do?

Foreign debts increased due to the depreciation of currencies. Companies closed down, or laid off people, or cut their employees' salary. The value of currencies had been halved. I can't bee anything positive.

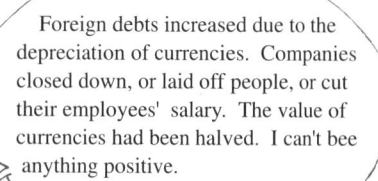

Because of the financial crisis, insolvent companies and banks will be weeded out. The businesses that have been under improperly favorable protection of governments will lose the shelter they are unworthy of and enter the fair competition in the market mechanism.

Just like the natural selection. The unfit will be phased out.

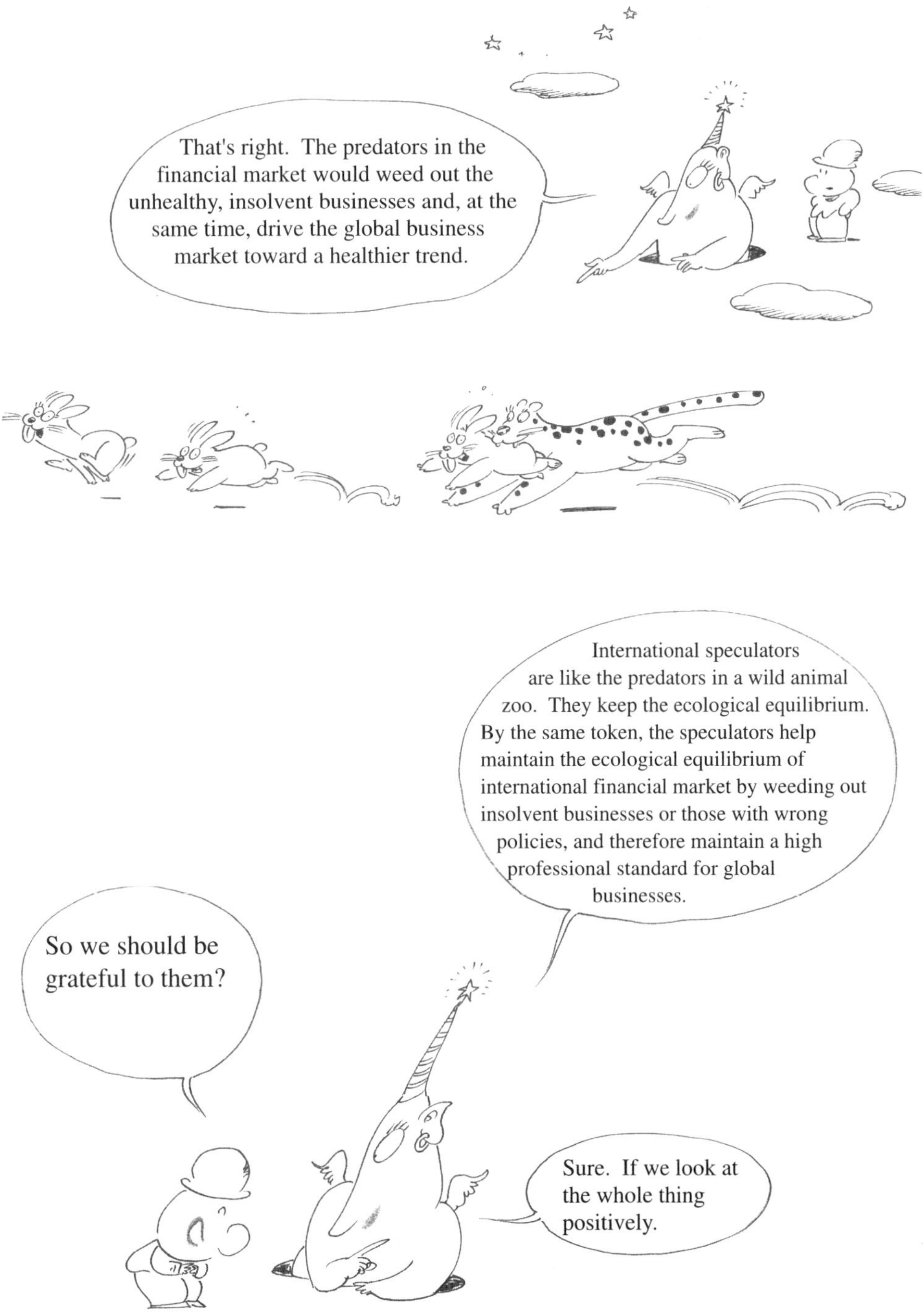
That's right. The predators in the financial market would weed out the unhealthy, insolvent businesses and, at the same time, drive the global business market toward a healthier trend.
International speculators are like the predators in a wild animal zoo. They keep the ecological equilibrium. By the same token, the speculators help maintain the ecological equilibrium of international financial market by weeding out insolvent businesses or those with wrong policies, and therefore maintain a high professional standard for global businesses.
So we should be grateful to them?
Sure. If we look at the whole thing positively.

4. East Asian Countries: Present Situation and Short-term Policy Response

Generally, Westerners know how to use their wealth in the most effective ways to ensure the benefits of that wealth. In contrast, most people in East Asia don't have many ideas about financial management. Most people in East Asia believe that they should have many houses and cars. After the financial crisis, building proper financial management concepts is a task of top priority.

Largo

Over the past six years, business necessity has led me to travel extensively throughout the East Asian region. In fact, during the course of one year I spent over 300 nights in the region's hotels, and thus feel that I have some knowledge of the region's inner-workings. My travels have also given me a strong sense of concern for the region's future. Over the past six months, to complete this book, I have continuously engaged in visits and interviews throughout the region, and have gathered a large volume of information, yet the more research I conducted, the more I felt that my knowledge on the subject was inadequate. Below, I include an overview of key statistics and important features of each of the key regional players in the current East Asian Financial Crisis. I regret that as my knowledge of the subject is limited, or as some issues are politically sensitive, I am constrained in my ability to provide a complete analysis of the situation in each East Asian country, but I nevertheless have done my best to provide as comprehensive a picture as possible.

What follows is a North to South discussion of each country's short-term policies in response to the

Crisis. (All economic information that follows, except for statistics on foreign currency reserves, are derived from the March 1998 issue of The International Chinese Newsweekly).

Map of East Asia

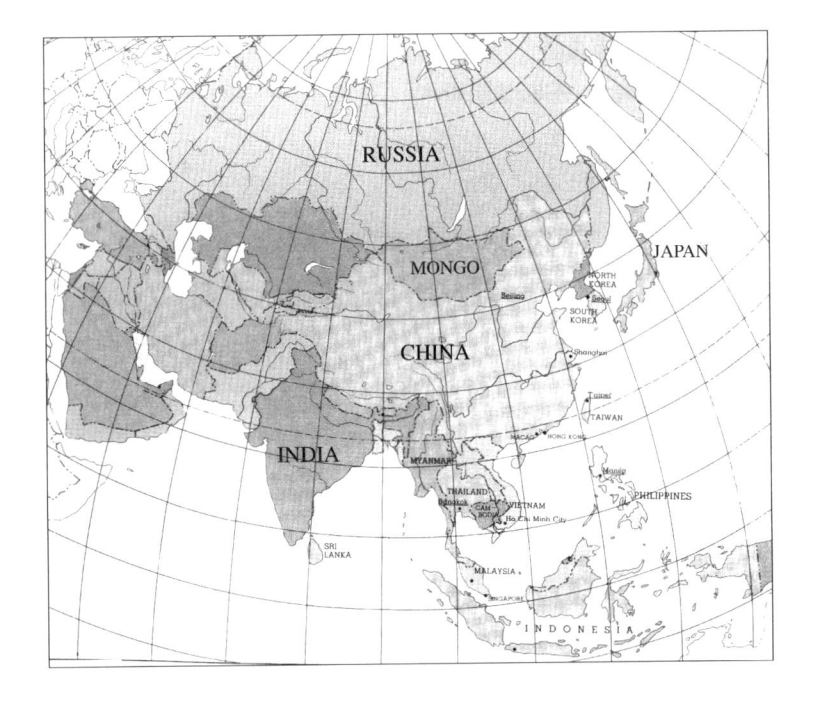

4.1   Japan

Area: 377,835 sq. km.
Population: 126.1m
GDP Per Capita: US$33,090
Exports: US$411bn
Trade Surplus: US$94.4bn
Foreign Exchange Reserves: US$216.65bn (1996)
External Debt: nil

According to Japanese legend, the Japanese Empire was formed in the 7th century B.C. A traceable historical thread, however, is only evident beginning from a time one thousand years later. With respect to culture, Chinese influences are strong, while in the area of religion, Buddhism was transmitted to Japan in the 6th Century A.D.

Beginning in 1192, Japan entered into the Vakuhu Period when internecine strife prevailed and only in 1868 after the Meiji Restoration was the country united. From the 16th to the 17th Century, the Portuguese and Dutch began to trade with Japan, while the US established commercial relations with Japan only after 1854. Japan acquired Formosa (Taiwan) in the Sino-Japanese War of 1894/95, and then following the Russo-Japanese War of 1904/05, Japan took the southern half of the Sakhalin and won treaty concessions from Russia in Northeastern China. In 1910, Japan annexed Korea.

Following the end of the First World War, Japan assumed the German concessions in Northeastern China, and won control over several German-held islands in the Pacific. Following the invasion of Manchuria in 1931, Japan then attacked Shanghai in 1932, and in 1937 entered into full-scale war in China. By 1941, Japan had fully entered into the Pacific War and following her defeat in that portion of the Second World War, surrendered unconditionally on August 14, 1945.

In May 1947, Japan amended its Constitution, and the Emperor became the sovereign only in name, while the Diet became the only body authorized to enact laws. In addition, the Constitution forbids Japan from ever again conducting war. Under protection of the US, Japan sought to aggressively develop its industry, and quickly became one of the wealthiest nations on the planet.

Japan is located at the extreme northern end of East Asia, and is widely recognised as the region's leading economic power. Owing, however, to the conservative and insular nature of the Japanese people as well as to the region's bitter memories of earlier Japanese aggression in Asia, Japan has never played a role in leading the region politically, nor has Japan seemed to harbour any desire to play a leadership role in the region. This is in contrast to the political leadership which the US has exerted among the nations of the West. Also unlike the US, Japan has never opened its markets to the nations of Southeast Asia. Japanese investment in East Asia has also been conducted with a view to leaving core technology and control in Japan. This again contrasts with the Western model whereby many corporations view the entire world as their base of operations.

Domestic Problems

Following Japan's defeat in World War II, Japan rebuilt herself thanks to generous assistance from the US as well as to the assiduous efforts of the Japanese people. During the Cold War period, Japan was able to focus almost exclusively on economic development for she did not have to support a standing Army. Beginning in the 1950's, then, the Japanese economy embarked on a dramatic upward ascent. In so doing, Japan also helped to boost economic growth in the "Four Dragons" of South Korea, Taiwan, Hong Kong, and Singapore. By the 1980's the Japanese economy had developed to its apex, and a "Japan as Number One" doctrine prevailed in some circles. The Japanese management style, including lifetime job security, zero inventory, quality circles, five S of quality, and other programs, became the focus of study and commentary for management experts the world over. Indeed, at the height of her economic might, Japan's economic achievements were almost the stuff of legend.

With the start of the 1990's, however, the Japanese economy began to undergo a seemingly inexorable slide. Always introspective, Japanese economic and management experts studied Japan's slide in great detail and searched for answers, yet to the present have been unable to formulate policies to stem the steady erosion in Japan's competitiveness.

Amongst Japan's many problems at present, two

stand out in particular. The first is Japan's loss of leadership in the electronics industry; while the second is the ageing of the Japanese management stratum.

The electronics industry had been the major factor of Japan's economic growth. Perhaps more importantly, going forward the electronics industry also represents one of the most important locomotives for growth in the global economy. During the latter part of the 1980's, many scholars in Japan echoed the slogan "Build the Nation through Electronics" . Unfortunately for Japan, it was precisely at that time that the US, through the global PC industry which the US leads, reasserted its dominance throughout the entire electronics industry.

Another problem for Japan was its system of lifetime employment. Once hired by a company, a worker in Japan was expected to remain his entire life with the company. Japanese companies employed fair practices with respect to promotion and salary increases. Employee loyalty in Japan was thus extremely high, and each worker tended to work very hard for the company to which he or she belonged. Workers also tended to have strong respect for their superiors, as the superior was key to the career advancement potential of the subordinate. It is not difficult to imagine that with a large number of new workers destined for lifetime employment with a company, given the strong dedication, motivation and work-ethic that the lifetime employment system instilled, such a system had very strong competitive advantages. Indeed this system was key in creating Japan's economic miracle of the 1960's, 70's and 80's. By the end of the 1980's, however, those same workers who had worked so hard to build Japan's economic success in the 1960's were now in their 60's and 70's and were employed in management, controlling the fate of the companies which they had nurtured and which had nurtured them.

It was at this point that the disadvantages of the lifetime employment system began to come to light. The most obvious drawback was the high overhead that the system entailed. In addition, the system promoted a conservative and relatively unresponsive management decision-making process. Opportunities for advancement were also stifled in many cases. Ageing of the workforce became especially severe in industries shielded from international competition, including the banking and securities industries. If these problems aren't addressed decisively in the near future, Japanese competitiveness and economic health are likely to continue to suffer.

Japanese investment in East Asia

Japan has invested considerable sums throughout East Asia. If Japan is not the largest foreign direct investor in most Asian countries, then it certainly ranks among the top few. In addition, Japanese businessmen throughout Asia tend to adopt a relatively low-profile, considered, and cooperative approach in working with governments in the region. Japanese companies in East Asia seldom withdraw capital from regions into which they have previously invested. Japanese investment patterns thus reflect the Japanese way of doing business, which emphasises harmony and long-term relations. As a result of these investment characteristics, we can easily deduce that Japanese investors in the region must have sustained heavy losses as a result of the East Asian Financial Crisis. Despite these losses, it is probably safe to say that Japanese companies will not pull back from the region unless absolutely forced to do so.

The Japanese Ability to Respond to the Current Crisis

During the current economic crisis, I have constantly asked one particular question: during the past ten to twenty years, Japan has encountered many instances of large currency fluctuation. In each case, the magnitude of fluctuation was on a par with the magnitude of the currency realignment. In previous instances why was the Japanese economy able to emerge relatively unharmed? It appeared in the past as though Japan indeed would always be able to deal conclusively with any currency crisis that might arise.

Recently, in line with the regional crisis, several Japanese securities companies have collapsed. As a result, many have criticized the Japanese government's handling of the crisis. Personally, I believe that the ageing of the corporate workforce in Japan is much more important in explaining the recent string of corporate failures than is the financial crisis.

What can Japan Do?

Provide to Neighbouring Countries Information on Accommodating Large-Scale Currency Fluctuations

After the economies of East Asia had grown to a

large enough size, they became unable to sustain a US dollar peg. Sooner or later, the region's currencies need to float against the US dollar, just as the currencies of Europe and Japan do. The most important contribution that Japan can make to the region is to provide to its East Asian neighbours Japan's long experience in managing the currency float.

Adjust its Investment Strategy in East Asia

The strategy governing Japanese investment in East Asia had previously been based on utilizing the region's cheap source of labour and to exploit opportunities in the regional markets. Going forward, Japan needs to focus on exporting technology and assisting neighbouring countries to develop their own bases of technology. In addition, Japan should transplant to East Asia its conventional industries, while focusing at home on concentrating on very high-end technology intensive industries. Only in this way can Japan help others and in the process also help itself.

Japan has always been a tightly knit society built on a sound foundation of skill and talent. In the past, it did not need to be outward looking. Her experts are well aware of the many problems with which Japan is now confronted. As Japan continues to involve itself in the region, however, the Japanese education system needs to boost training in foreign languages, for in the past Japanese often had difficulty communicating with the rest of Asia. This is another problem which Japan should address as soon as possible.

4.2   Korea

Area: 98,480 sq. km.
Population: 46.1m
GPD Per Capita: US$10,730
Exports: US$140bn
Trade Deficit: US$2.8bn
Foreign Exchange Reserves: US$33.24bn (1996)

Historical records in Korea date back to the first century B.C. Korea was annexed by China in 668 A.D. From 1894 to 1895, both China and Japan recognized the independence of the Korean Peninsula. Korea, however, was forcibly incorporated into Japan in 1910.

Following Japan's defeat in World War II, the Potsdam Agreement provided for the division of the Korean Peninsula into Northern and Southern halves occupied by the Soviet Union and the United States, respectively. The 38th parallel served as the demarcation line between the two halves. Shortly after the division, the Soviets established a puppet regime in the North and blocked the reunification of the two Koreas.

In May of 1948, the South Koreans established the nation of Korea, with its capital in Seoul and in August officially declared the establishment of the Republic of Korea with Rhee Syng Man as the first President. When making reference to Korea in the context of the East Asian Financial Crisis, the reference is typically to South Korea.

It is worth noting at this point that North Korea, similar to the Taiwan of twenty or thirty years ago, maintains very tight controls on capital and foreign exchange. The populace cannot easily exchange the North Korean currency for US dollars. Previously we had emphasised that following liberalization and internationalization of the regional financial markets, currency markets had become the world's largest and most attractive capital markets in the eyes of speculators and investors. The national currency thus became tantamount to the nation's "equity" in those nations which maintained freely convertible currencies. As "equity", currencies thus became subject to increased volatility. Those countries that maintained strict capital controls, however, were able to much better avoid the unsettling effects of the currency crisis. It is for this reason that North Korea is seldom

mentioned in the context of the East Asian Financial
Crisis.

Current Situation and Problems

With respect to its population and the scale of its
industry, Korea tends to be placed at the "head" of
the Four Dragons. Many of Korea's largest
corporations compare favourably in size with large
corporations in the US, Europe and Japan. Among
these, Samsung ranks within the top-30 corporations
worldwide, ranking even ahead of Toshiba. Given
Korea's cold and isolated climate, the Korean people
have developed a rugged and determined spirit, and
are also known for their strong sense of unity. In
addition, relative to other Asian peoples, the Koreans
are known for being tough and somewhat hot-blooded.
Other traits generally associated with Koreans include
a strong sense of self-respect and an unwillingness to
accept defeat.

Over the past thirty to forty years, Korean
development strategy has focused on Japan as the
chief competitor. Once a Korean company had
identified its key Japanese competitor, it typically
sought to take advantage of Korea's low labour costs

to compete on price with the competition. From the standpoint of the Japanese, Korea has always been a dangerous opponent as well as a force prompting Japan to continually upgrade its own industrial base. To catch up with Japan, the Korean government and Korean corporations worked hand-in-hand at times often subsidizing exports through higher prices at home. These practices, however, also came with inherent difficulties attached.

In a market economy, the role of the corporation is to create wealth. The government's role is to distribute wealth. In addition to supporting the nation's businesses, the government must also play a supervisory role. When the government and corporate sector work closely, such cooperation can certainly speed industrial development. If these two key actors in the economy work too closely together, however, then corruption can easily become an important problem. The famous phrase "absolute power breeds absolute corruption" warns us that IF corrupt practices are hidden by those in authority, over time such practices can lead to seriously negative consequences.

Throughout its recent past, Japan also adopted a

structure whereby the ruling party worked closely with financial interests toward the aim of social order and stable economic development. In the initial phase of Japan's post-war economic development, such cooperation produced impressive results. However, in the end, the long-term effects of persistent corruption finally led to the collapse of the ruling Liberal Democratic Party, in turn causing political disarray. Luckily for Japan, her industrial base had already been secured by the time that political disarray became manifest. The results of political turmoil were thus relatively unimportant to the economy. In addition, aside from a reliance on large corporations, the Japanese economy also derived strength from a broad base of medium-sized and small corporations which provided economic stability.

Political and economic systems in Korea tend to emulate those of Japan. As Korea got its start later than did Japan, however, Korean companies which sought to capture Japanese market share in overseas markets were forced to pay a heavy price. Profits thus were typically thin, and added to this, excessive protection from the Korean government meant that Korean corporations tended to have a less stable base than might otherwise have been the case in the absence of government support. As Korea also neglected to develop a strong base of medium- and small- sized enterprises, the Korean economy came to be dependent on a relatively small number of companies with relatively weak international competitiveness. Given the size of many Korean corporations, and given strong government support, it was furthermore quite easy for such corporations to raise capital overseas. The combination of heavy debt and low profitability, however, locked such corporations into a cycle of indebtedness. Against this backdrop, given widespread government corruption, regulatory authorities were unable to fully prevent the spiral of debt from widening beyond permissible limits.

The reason Korea became the focal point in North Asia of the regional crisis is relatively simple: Korea's external debt exceeded its foreign exchange reserves. In addition, the external debt reported by the government was lower by three-fold than the amount which eventually came to light.

Blind expansion, misguided export subsidisation and gross indebtedness all combined to drag Korea head first into the regional economic crisis. Korea's involvement in the crisis also reveals that Korean corporations violated the prime law of corporate strategy - corporate development strategy should not be based on the goal of directly competing with competitors, but rather should be based on the goal of developing one's own competitive advantages in the interest of achieving the highest possible returns.

Short-term Policy Response

I have visited Korea on several occasions in the past and have always been impressed with the determination and ambition of the Korean people. My strong feeling is that the Koreans will quickly regain their lost economic momentum. Always deeply patriotic, Koreans have responded eagerly to the call to donate US dollars and gold to the government. Given such dramatic efforts, with proper assistance from the IMF and as long as the Korean people remain calm and recover confidence in the won, the crisis in Korea can surely end soon.

To bring about a speedy resolution to the crisis, however, the Korean corporate sector must also strive to change its operating strategy. Compared with other East Asian countries outside Japan, Korea's biggest advantage is that it already has a number of world-class, internationally competitive companies. As long as Korean corporations continue to focus on their core competencies, such companies should be in a strong competitive position.

In the past annals of global economic activity, large companies sought diversification, whereas small companies sought specialization. In other words, it meant that large corporations used their sufficient capital and resources to diversify their operations, and small corporations used their limited resources to focus on certain industries. One key change evident in the 1990s is that large companies are now also seeking specialization. Indeed, many large corporations are seeking to place their considerable resources in relatively narrow sets of industries in the hope of becoming the world leader in their chosen categories. Companies which have followed such a model include Microsoft, Intel, Nintendo and others. In the most simplistic terms, if Korean corporations can take advantage of the lessons learned in the East Asian Financial Crisis and redouble efforts to restructure and re-align corporate aims in favour of specialization, Korea may not only quickly recover

from the crisis. It may actually emerge from the crisis
in a stronger position than it had been prior to the
Asian financial turmoil.

4.3   China

Area: 9,596,960 sq. km.
Population: 1,236.26m
GDP Per Capita: US$655
Exports: US$151bn
Trade Surplus: US$7.2bn
Foreign Exchange Reserves: US$107.03bn (1996)
External Debt: US$116.28bn

The PRC (People's Republic of China) was established in 1949. Since 1978, Mainland China has developed through the reformist policies put forward by former Communist Party Chairman, Deng Xiao-ping. It was Deng's open-door policy that helped to attract large amounts of foreign investment to Mainland China. Recently, Chinese businessmen from Hong Kong, Taiwan, and Singapore have continued to invest funds and technology in China so that the economy has evolved from its past socialist roots to become a more open market economy. As a result, Mainland China's inhabitants have seen remarkable advances in their standard of living.

After receiving a setback following the government crackdown in Tiananmen Square in 1989, the mainland economy has subsequently posted impressive growth in the 1990s. At the end of 1997, foreign exchange reserves amounted to US$140bn while the trade surplus amounted to US$40bn. For a country with such a large population, China has done particularly well to maintain its economic growth rate at 10% for the past few years. Currently, it is one of the world's few growth engines.

Current situation and problems

After almost twenty years of operating under an open-door policy, China's cities have undergone a profound transformation. Under this policy, the government has given priority to the development of three specific areas: transportation, energy (resources), and telecommunications. New inter-provincial highways and airports have been built, the world's largest water power station - the San Xia Engineering project - is currently close to completion, and the pace of development in the telecommunications sector has been impressive with the number of phone lines increasing by an average of 10m per year and the number of pagers currently almost equal to the number in the US. In 1992, there were about 100,000 mobile phones in China but by 1997 that number had grown to exceed 10m.

Cheap labour, a well-educated and diligent workforce, skilled engineers, and a huge domestic market have attracted foreign investors to the country in droves. In total, cumulative foreign investment in China now amounts to US$360bn, of which US$220bn is in the form of FDI and the remainder in the form of long term debt and short term foreign investment. Foreign debt and foreign exchange reserves are broadly equivalent and generally speaking, the outlook for the mainland economy is quite good.

However, there are also serious problems that China needs to resolved if it is to avoid economic slowing. The most obvious one is the vexing issue of what to do with the nation's state-owned enterprises. Since opening up its markets, China has benefited from US$220bn in FDI and this has helped to stimulate economic development throughout the country. At the same time, it has made redundant a huge number of state-owned factories, which are no longer competitive. This is a serious problem for mainland authorities as they seek to avoid spiraling unemployment while shutting down out-dated factories.

State-owned enterprises must not only confront the same problems that aging enterprises face the world over, but must also face the problems associated with the nation's transformation from a planned economy to a market economy. Of the tax revenues the government collects each year from the more than 100,000 state-run corporations in China, the 1,000 largest account for 80% of total receipts. Thus, while tax receipts will not be greatly affected even if the remaining state-run companies cease to operate, the crucial issue is what will happen to the tens of million employees currently working at state-owned enterprises.

Secondly, China has three main financial problems : high bad debt, the need to speed financial securitization, and the prevalence of underground financing.

The third biggest problem that Mainland China faces is in the private sector. Many private enterprises have not yet developed a source of wealth-creation. Most private enterprises on the mainland compete in the domestic market and have a short-term outlook. They tend to be large conglomerates with a lack of focus and are unable to compete internationally. It is rare to find a company in China with a well-defined, long-term strategy and which is willing to devote time to the development of markets overseas. In light of this, it is clear that economic development in China, to a large extent, has been triggered by an influx of foreign capital.

The fourth largest problem for China is its over-investment in consumption activities. New department stores, fast food outlets, discotheques, KTVs, golf courses and apartments have sprung up rapidly throughout the country. This contrasts sharply with the images we see on the news of workers struggling to survive. Many experts have pointed out that the problem of over-investment in China is very similar to that previously seen in Thailand.

Exchange rate policy

One of the main factors behind the regional crisis was Mainland China's increased export competitiveness over the past five to six years. This squeezed out exports from the region's other countries, and caused those countries to run up large trade deficits (including in The Philippines, Thailand, Malaysia, and Indonesia). The average wage in China is lower than that in any of these countries yet the quality and efficiency of the labour force is equivalent. With its huge domestic market, China is a strong competitor for the newly developed industrial countries in Southeast Asia. To prevent latent trade conflicts, China has decided to cancel certain concessions and incentives to its exporters, including tariff-free import of production equipment and reduction of tax refunds on goods sold in export markets.

Since the crisis, the Thai Baht, Philippine Peso, Indonesian Rupiah, and Malaysian Ringgit have fallen by between 40% to 70% against the US dollar. However, China continues to insist that it will not depreciate the renminbi. Experts differ as to whether the currency is likely to depreciate in the near future. However, the renminbi is not yet a fully convertible currency, and as such, is less vulnerable to attack from speculators. China's foreign reserves total US$140bn. In addition, China controls domestic inflation in a different manner than most countries. As a result, the decision as to whether to depreciate the renminbi will almost totally be up to the Chinese government.

Generally speaking, it should be more appropriate to maintain the renminbi at its current level as it is not clear that China would gain from a weaker currency. If the renminbi depreciates, other currencies in East Asia would most likely also suffer from a further round of currency depreciation. Any depreciation would also have a significant effect on the global economy, as the population in China is equal to the total population of North America and of all the European countries combined.

However, if China insists on not depreciating the renminbi, it is likely to see weakness in exports, a slow-down in foreign investment, and a reduction in its economic growth rate. So far, the current macro-economic situation in China remains healthy. As long as the economy is managed correctly, for example, promoting an upgrade in industries and increasing favorable policies for export industries, this is unlikely to change. After all, government policy over the past decade has been the main reason behind the country's rapid economic growth. Compared with medium and small-sized companies in Hong Kong and Taiwan, national enterprises and new private enterprises in

China have not had to face many difficulties when operating their businesses. Thus, the negative effects of not depreciating the renminbi can in some ways also be viewed in a positive manner.

Short-term policy response

China has a huge population. Naturally, therefore, there are a large number of talented people who can assist China in its future development. I have read the dissertations of many experts and scholars from the mainland and have learned a great deal from doing so. In my view, there are two themes which recur time and time again when one speaks of economic development in China.

In the wake of the recent crisis, China, like other countries in East Asia, will need to improve upon the weakness in its financial systems. I suggest two short-term strategies that may be suitable: firstly, adopt a policy of import substitution, and secondly, I would seek to develop intellectual economy.

The domestic market is well established in China during the process of the reformation. Although much statistical information and transaction order in the domestic market still need to be improved, the demand for the domestic market is easily planned. Henceforth, the onus on the government will be to encourage greater participation in international trade and to replace exports where possible with locally produced goods, thus reducing dependence on foreign currency. Meanwhile, it should avoid blind expansion, vicious competition, and unnecessary spending. In this way, China could reduce impact caused by the financial crisis like the current one in the process of liberalization and internationalization.

The second strand of this policy would be to develop intellectual economy. Agriculture-based economies are based on the use of limited resources to create wealth, while the industrial economy is centred around the increased use of science and technology. Some economists go so far as to call the agriculture-based economies, labour economies, and the industrial economies, resource economies. The information age that has now emerged is dubbed the intellectual economy by these economists, and this new information economy is defined by the use of knowledge to produce wealth.

Since the emergence of Bill Gates, who started from scratch to become the richest man in the world in a period of twenty years, we are living in an era where wealth can be created through the use of knowledge. As stated, the population in mainland China is huge and this 'resource' place China in a strong position as the information age gathers pace. The development of an intellectual economy is different from the development of a labour or resource economy, however in many key respects. In a labour economy, the elderly are unable to contribute owing to the physical nature of work; in a resource economy, increased integration also sees senior people cast aside as the pace becomes too demanding. In the information age, as long as one possesses knowledge, a computer, and a minimum in telecommunications equipment, one can contribute immensely to economic activity at anytime, regardless of age or location.

An American friend of mine recently told me that his mother would turn seventy-five years old soon. He told me that he called her up and asked her what she wanted as a present. His mother replied : " I want Windows 98 and more memory." In America, even the elderly have become as addicted to computers as children and housewives, if not more so. Indeed, research indicates that those who type frequently are least likely to suffer from Alzheimer's disease. Furthermore, through computers, the wisdom of the elderly can be appreciated and applied to new economic activities.

The intellectual economy will not restrict itself to computer related activities only, however, and activities such as writing a book, recording, orally dictating history, or any intellectual services can all be carried out more efficiently in the new information age. As for China, the more aggressive development of the intellectual economy will have the effect of turning the burden of having a large population into an advantage. Pursuing this strategy will help China solve its unemployment problems and help lead it into the new millennium.

4.4   Hong Kong

Area: 1,040 sq. km.
Population: 6.6m
GDP Per Capita: US$24,445
Exports: US$187bn
Trade Surplus: US$2.1bn
Foreign Exchange Reserves: US$63.8bn (1996)
External Debt: nil

The area we call Hong Kong includes the island of Hong Kong, Kowloon, and the New Territories, which were ceded to England in a series of treaties during the late nineteenth century. The Treaty of Nanking in 1842 was the first of these treaties and made Hong Kong island a British colony. The Treaty of Beijing followed the Treaty of Nanking in 1860 in which Kowloon Island came under British rule, and finally the New Territories Lease which gave England a ninety-nine year lease on the New Territories.

Hong Kong is one of only two duty free ports in Asia including Singapore and is one of the region's most vibrant economies. Since the Korean War, Hong Kong has been Mainland China's largest transshipment centre and its largest consumer market. Where Shanghai was once praised as the Paris of the East, Hong Kong is often called the Pearl of the Orient.

Britain and China signed an international agreement in 1984 which set the terms for the transition of Hong Kong back to Chinese rule on July 1, 1997.

It was under the benign neglect of British colonial rule that the hard work of millions of Chinese helped to make the colony into a world renowned economic miracle, as well as the largest financial centre in Asia outside of Japan. Hong Kong developed its own culture, a mixture of east and West, and a unique identity which exemplified the business acumen of the Hong Kong people. In an environment of low taxes and limited (some would say efficient), government (if such a thing is possible) Hong Kong flourished and became the shopper's paradise of Asia.

Over the last ten years, in line with mainland China's policy of economic reform, Hong Kong became the key transshipment centre for trade between Taiwan and China as well as the primary port for the fast developing Pearl River Delta region in the southern part of Guangdong Province. Commercial development was accompanied by an active popular culture which made Hong Kong a trend-setter for modern Asia. One example of this is the way in which the creativity and dynamism of Hong Kong's vibrant pop culture attracted the attention of the West and top US film schools began to devote courses to Hong Kong movies while Hong Kong actors and directors became involved in mainstream Hollywood productions.

Current situation and problems

In a moment which was at once exuberant and tense, on July 1, 1997, Hong Kong returned to Chinese rule under the One Country, Two Systems policy developed under the late Chairman of the Chinese Communist Party, Mr. Deng Xiao-ping. Cultural heritage not withstanding, it was the immense gap between the socialist culture which existed in mainland China and Hong Kong's capitalist culture which led Deng Xiao-ping to opt for the "One country-two, systems, no change for 50 years" policy which began its trial last year.

The advent of the Asian currency crisis in 1997 forced Hong Kong to defend its currency, which is pegged to the US dollar. Maintaining its own currency is in line with the new system which was intended to allow self-rule and a kind of virtual autonomy for Hong Kong even though the territory is now under Chinese rule. If Hong Kong did not enjoy special status, it would use the renminbi and therefore be exempt from defending the Hong Kong dollar peg following the Asian currency crisis.

While the Hong Kong dollar may be independent from Beijing, the determination of the Hong Kong central bank to defend the peg is now considered a leading indicator of the degree to which China will act to maintain the value of the renminbi. This view on the part of international investors is mainly due to the fact that the largest portion of China's trade with the outside world is through Hong Kong. The major difference between the Hong Kong dollar and the renminbi, however, is that the Hong Kong dollar is a hard currency which is freely traded and as such, its defense in the face of diminished confidence among local residents and attacks from currency speculators is seen as a tremendous test of the central bank's resolve.

The pressures brought about by the East Asian Financial Crisis illustrate the true meaning of the One Country, Two Systems policy. Though it boasts the largest concentration of financial professionals and institutions in Asia ex-Japan, Hong Kong is subject to all of the vagaries and uncertainty associated with international markets and the territory's government must act independently to maintain the integrity of its systems. At the same time, when the territory encounters financial challenges or difficulties, it is important that Hong Kong and China cooperate as one country to meet these challenges. The ability to cooperate with mainland China while at the same time maintaining independence exemplifies the spirit of the One Country, Two Systems policy now in place.

The primary cost to Hong Kong of defending the peg has been reflected in reduced domestic consumption and falling receipts from tourism. Together, these problems have led to a decline in economic growth. Domestic consumption declined as consumer confidence collapsed along with sharp drops in the local stock and property markets. Tourism in Hong Kong declined due to the relatively high expense of Hong Kong versus other Asian countries and fear of disease in the aftermath of the Chicken Flu epidemic which broke out in the summer of 1997. The decline in domestic consumption and tourism, and accompanying slower growth, have been a bitter price for Hong Kong to pay in the wake of the Asian financial crisis.

An additional potential threat to the Hong Kong economy is a decline in trade as the effects of a relatively expensive renminbi are reflected in Chinese trade figures. The approaching advent of direct links between China and Taiwan also threatens Hong Kong's status as an entrepot to China. As the industrial centre of southern China, it is still uncertain how much the Pearl River Delta region will be affected by the enormous decline in currency values among its chief competitors in South East Asia. As currency values in the region stabilize, most observers feel that a decline in Chinese exports is likely without a devaluation of the renminbi. At the same time Hong Kong's position as the major transshipment centre between Taiwan and Mainland China will remain under pressure as direct shipping links across the Taiwan Straits continues to develop.

Short-term policy response

Assuming that the Hong Kong economy will recover its previous health, I believe that perhaps the most important work of the Hong Kong people remains to develop a stronger relationship with mainland China under the One Country, Two Systems policy. While the impact of the Asian financial crisis is sure to be felt, economic recovery in Hong Kong seems ensured thanks to the sharp business acumen of the Hong Kong people. England's former Prime Minister Margaret Thatcher once called Hong Kongers "born traders". Indeed, like a cat with nine lives under British rule the colony had a history of bouncing back from economic adversity time and again. Going forward, the degree to which it is able to adapt to the one country, two systems policy, its ability to find new models of commercial and industrial development, and its close relationship with the mainland, (perhaps enhanced by an increased study of Mandarin) are the keys to Hong Kong's future.

4.5   Taiwan

Area: 35,980 sq. km.
Population: 21.7m
GDP Per Capita: US$12,265
Exports: US$122bn
Trade Surplus: US$7.4bn
Foreign Exchange Reserves: US$88.04bn (1996)
External Debt: nil

During the 16th and 17th Centuries, Portuguese and Spanish traders that saw Taiwan, called her "Ilha Formosa", or the "Beautiful Island". In 1624, the Dutch invaded Taiwan and established a colony, ruling the island for 37 years. In 1626, the Spanish invaded northern Taiwan, but were pushed out 16 years later by the Dutch, whereupon in 1661, displaced Ming official Cheng Cheng-kung forced out the Dutch and used Taiwan as a base in an unsuccessful bid to defeat the Ching invaders and restore the Ming Dynasty.

In 1895, after losing to Japan in the Sino-

Japanese War, the Ching rulers in China signed the Treaty of Shimonoseki which ceded Taiwan to Japan and marked the beginning of 50 years of Japanese colonial rule in Taiwan. Only in 1945 was Taiwan returned to China.

Current Situation and Problems

Taiwan is fortunate to have escaped the brunt of the East Asian Financial Crisis. Taiwan in fact is seen by many as a land of great promise. In particular, while the Taiwanese financial system is not as transparent and structured as are systems found in Singapore and Hong Kong, Taiwan's financial system is, nevertheless, much sounder than those of other East Asian countries. Past fiscal and economic policy in Taiwan is similar in many ways to that of Mainland China: it is characterized by an attempt at steady and gradual liberalization and internationalization. Following political relaxation and easing of controls on the press, demands for liberalization have grown in Taiwan, and the pace of opening up has thus steadily gained momentum.

In the final analysis, there are three key reasons why Taiwan has been able to avoid significant setbacks in connection with the recent financial turmoil. The first has to do with Taiwan's very sound economic fundamentals. The island enjoys a large accumulation of foreign reserves and has no net external debt. The second is linked to Taiwan's plentiful supply of experienced and capable banking and financial professionals. As unlike in Japan or Korea, the Taiwanese economy has been built mainly upon a base of medium and small-sized companies, Taiwanese banking officials are accustomed to dealing with a wide variety of difficult banking problems. The final reason explaining Taiwan's economic success is linked to the solid wealth creation system which underpins the island's economy, especially with respect to the island's highly-competitive manufacturing sector.

In the past, I have many times delivered speeches in banks, and banking officers have often asked me questions such as "what should I do if the customer is not willing to open an invoice?" I usually answered that most banking officials themselves have worked in medium or small businesses and they should be very familiar with business practices in such firms. Even Taiwan's Central Bankers have typically worked their way through the "School of Hard Knocks". Taiwan's bankers are thus extremely well-equipped to deal with problems that arise in the trading of foreign currencies and in other areas.

Perhaps the third reason for Taiwan's economic success - a strong manufacturing base -is the most important reason of all. In all areas of manufacturing from agricultural-related production, to industrial production, to production in the information industry, the tireless and teamwork-oriented approach of the Taiwanese worker, coupled with the continuous drive towards innovation and satisfying the customer's needs, allows Taiwanese industry to work closely and successfully with its European, American, and Japanese customers. This forms the basis of Taiwan's value creation system. In addition, that such a small island as Taiwan can produce exports in excess of US$100bn to supplement a stockpile of foreign currency reserves topping US$80bn means that Taiwan has been able to avoid the direct impact of the East Asian Financial Crisis.

Taiwan's relatively large manufacturing base in conventional industry, including textiles, petrochemicals, steel, food products continue to enjoy a strong competitive position. Taiwan's medium and small businesses, on the other hand, have steadily lost competitiveness owing to increasing costs at home and have thus relocated in droves to mainland China and other Asian nations. By relocating, such companies not only have been able to maintain competitiveness, but also have been able to contribute strongly to growth in other neighbouring countries. Taiwan's success came not just in transplanting its less competitive sectors overseas, but also in working to swiftly upgrade its industrial base at home. Indeed, Taiwan's electronics industry, led by the PC and IC industries, already accounts for over 25% of the island's total exports. Furthermore, Taiwan's success in developing its electronics sector has attracted a large number of the island's young people to the industry and has also attracted back to the island a large number of overseas entrepreneurs and engineers. Future prospects for the Taiwan electronics sector, thus, are excellent.

Despite the overall rosy picture, Taiwan is not without its problems. In particular, there are three large problems which require attention.

The first problem is Taiwan's uncertain political

relationship with Mainland China. At no time since the 1949 split between Taiwan and Mainland China have private contact between Taiwan and the mainland been so intensive as at present. Economic reliance across the Taiwan Straits is also growing daily. While each side is clearly capable of undertaking economic development independent of the other, no one in government or academia has yet come up with a convincing argument against unleashing the powerful economic synergies inherent in the cross-Strait relationship. Despite this fact, political reconciliation across the Taiwan-Strait has been slow in coming, and this fact represents a major variable in an otherwise bright picture for Taiwan's future economic development. In addition, the lack of political accord means that Taiwanese investors in China continue to suffer from a sense of unease. Greater political will is needed to solve this vexing and important problem.

A second problem which Taiwan faces is that political activities in Taiwan exhaust enormous societal resources. Over the past ten years, Taiwanese society has undergone major changes. The island has transformed itself from a one party-system into a multiparty democracy. In the course of this change, marked by establishment of freedoms for the press and political association and opening of the airwaves, a public unaccustomed to such freedoms has at times found difficulty in making the adjustment to democracy. Political turmoil typically sets in around the time of elections, when commentators fan the flames of public opinion and even husbands and wives become embroiled on opposite sides of political feuds. As the prime purpose of government is to create laws to govern conduct in the society, there is no reason for society to spend so much capital in the interest of "political exhibitionism".

The third major problem which Taiwan confronts is the knowledge gap that exists between the various strata in society. As Taiwan underwent an extremely rapid fifty-year development from an agrarian to industrial society, gaps have emerged between those raised in the agrarian period, those raised in the industrial period, and those raised in the information age. Given Taiwan's small land area, such gaps can lead to social friction. It is perhaps this phenomenon which has led to a deterioration in the social order in Taiwan of late. The deterioration to which we refer includes rising crime, prevalence of financial games and get-rich-quick schemes, and a growing division between rich and poor. Rapid economic growth in Taiwan has created significant wealth on the island, yet given the gap in knowledge that divides elements of society, the differing strata in society often take divergent approaches to disposing the island's new found wealth. Many see the increase in wealth on the island as causing a breakdown in traditional values. Others point to the fact that the island's lower classes are sometimes unable to properly manage their newfound wealth, and thus despite improvements in the standard of living, are still reduced to borrowing and indebtedness. Relative poverty is not necessarily a function of insufficient income, but rather of expenditures which exceed the capacity to earn.

Short-term policy response

The first response should be to aggressively seek to improve cross-strait relations. Taiwan and Mainland China have already been divided for 50 years. While Taiwanese and Mainland Chinese speak the same language and share a common ethnicity, the fifty-year divide has produced a divergence in thoughts and ideas. To seek a way forward, both sides must attempt first to find and build common ground in values and ideas.

The second response should be to plug the knowledge gap that separates the various strata in Taiwanese society. At present, Taiwanese society can be characterised as being too rich in information, but too poor in knowledge. The success of televised political debates suggests that people are thirsty for knowledge. How to broadly disseminate knowledge throughout all levels of the society (and not simply through the public media) is one of the largest challenges now facing the government.

The third response to Taiwan's current problems lies in the integration of PCs and ICs. As the Asian nations nurse the wounds sustained as a result of the East Asian Financial Crisis, each is bound to redouble efforts to promote export-led industrial development. In line with this trend, Taiwan can work to aggressively transplant to Mainland China and other Asian nations the island's conventional industry. Taiwan should then focus on intensive integration and development of its IC and PC industries, industries where the island already enjoys a strong competitive advantage. Taiwan has already invested considerable sums in developing its electronics industries, yet investment in the PC industry has focused on importing key components and raw materials for mid- and down- stream assembly and re-export on behalf of major international OEMs. The IC industry is also established on a base emphasising foundry (OEM) services. If Taiwan seeks to become a leader in the global high-tech sector, it must seek to integrate and develop its PC and IC sectors.

4.6   Philippines

Area: 300,000 sq. km.
Population: 72.6m
GDP Per Capita: US$1,130
Exports: US$25.2bn
Trade Deficit: US$3.5bn
Foreign Exchange Reserves: US$10.03bn (1996)
External Debt: US$39.4bn

The original inhabitants of the Philippines were Malay, who probably settled in the island chain after leaving Southeast Asia. The early inhabitants subsisted mainly through hunting and fishing. The first Europeans to arrive were Muslims, who mainly settled in the southern islands of the island chain. Magellan came to the Philippines in 1521, and in 1571 the Spanish established Manila, and the islands from that point were named the "Philippines" in honour of the Spanish monarch Philip II.

After the US defeated Spain in the Spanish-American War of 1898, the US took control of the

Philippines from Spain. The Americans then fought a seven-year guerilla conflict against local insurgents before finally pacifying the populace. During World War II, Japan gained control over the Philippines during a period stretching from 1941 to 1942. Following Japan's defeat in World War II, the Japanese Army withdrew from the Philippines in September, 1945. The Philippines declared independence on July 4, 1946.

As The Philippines has previously been under American rule, the islands' political system closely mirrors an American-style democracy. In addition, English is spoken widely throughout the country. The people of the Philippines are warm and hard-working, and there are many cultural affinities between the Philippines and the US.

Current Situation and Problems.

With respect to economic development The Philippines enjoys a number of advantages over Thailand, Malaysia, Indonesia, and other Asian countries. In particular, The Philippines enjoys a superior geographic position as well as the benefit of a strong capability in the English language.

Unfortunately, political instability and high crime rates meant that the Philippines never benefited from the waves of FDI that swept the region in the late 1980's. Thus among the ASEAN four, the Philippines had a relatively late start in terms of its economic development.

Over the past three to four years, the political situation in the Philippines has steadily improved. Levels of FDI have steadily increased. Unfortunately, however, just at a time when the economy was headed in promising directions, the country suddenly found itself in the midst of the East Asian Financial Crisis. As the Philippine Peso is freely convertible, the currency came under attack by speculators and investors shortly after the Thai Baht was devalued in July 1997. While the Peso fell by roughly 40% in value over a short period, the Philippines nevertheless sustained less economic damage than did Thailand, Malaysia, and Indonesia.

As the Philippines has been influenced by consumption patterns in the US, the saving rate in the Philippines is relatively low when compared with rates in other Asian nations. In addition, as the Philippines has been under long-term IMF supervision, the financial sector in the Philippines is relatively stable. Given the islands' later start in economic development, foreign investment levels within the country and external debt were also lower than those seen in neighbouring countries. As a result, the Philippines did not suffer from the same level of over-investment that plagued other Asian countries. The 40% depreciation of the currency has also allowed the Philippines to maintain export competitiveness with other neighbouring countries. At this point, we also point out that the magnitude of depreciation of a currency does not directly correlate to the degree of economic damage an economy sustains in the course of a currency crisis. The number of bankruptcies which follow the currency crisis, the degree of stagnation in economic growth, the rise in unemployment - these are the economic indicators which measure damage to an economy beset by financial turmoil. If currency depreciation is not followed by deterioration in economic fundamentals - European currencies fluctuate daily against the US dollar - then currency depreciation does not necessarily point to economic weakness or damage.

The main impact on the Philippines of the East

Asian Financial Crisis may only be seen in the longer term. In particular, the Philippines is a country badly in need of foreign investment and the crisis is bound to reduce capital inflows into the islands for some time to come. In addition, questions remain as to whether the army of overseas Filipino workers in Asia will suffer from the regional economic slowdown and are sent back to the Philippines to join the rolls of the unemployed.

Short-term Policy Response

The first response should be to seek political stability and reduce crime. Over the past ten years, perceived political instability and high crime rates have meant that potential foreign investors have been slow to invest in the Philippines. Over the most recent three or four years, the situation has improved dramatically. Following this year's presidential elections, if newly-elected President Estrada can continue to achieve political stability and fight crime, this should help to ensure that the Philippines economy will not suffer a serious setback.

The second response should be to seek to develop the Internet services industry. Given the islanders' native strengths in the English language, Filipinos find it easy to find work throughout Asia. Many Asian parents even use their Filipina maids to teach English to their children. The Philippines should seek to exploit native advantages in English proficiency to develop a Philippine niche in the Internet services industry, especially in areas such as English instruction, after-sales service, training, and other areas. In this way, the Philippines can earn badly-needed hard currency and reduce the current account deficit.

4.7   Thailand

Size: 513,115 sq. km.
Population: 61.4m
GDP Per Capita: US$2,680
Exports: US$58.5bn
Trade Deficit: US$3.2bn
Foreign Exchange Reserves: US$37.73bn (1996)
External Debt: US$92.9bn

Today's modern Thais moved to Thailand from Southern China in the 11th Century A.D. Thailand is the only Southeast Asian country that was never colonized by the European powers. Credit for development of Thailand largely goes to Mongkut and Chulalongkorn, Thai kings who ruled from 1851 to 1910. Both kings promoted modernization in Thailand and signed trade agreements with England and France.

Thailand is located in the center of the Indo-China Peninsula. The land is fertile, crops are plentiful, and foreign invasion has been rare. The Thai people are devout Buddhists, and are known for their tolerance and love of peace. The majority of foreigners who have moved to Thailand, including the 20% of the population of Chinese ancestry, tend to intermarry with the local Thais and are easily accepted into the harmonious Thai society.

While Thailand has adopted a model of government based on a constitutional monarchy, one difference with other constitutional monarchies is that the King of Thailand enjoys a revered status among all levels of society and at crucial moments the King has powers to make political decisions.

Current Situation and Problems

From a Western point of view, the country's political foundations are unsound at best. Thai society is governed by relationships, friendships and emotion, rather than by the rule of law and application of logic. At New Year, traffic police openly accept gifts from pedestrians and motorists, and at times such gifts can even occupy the entire safety island on which the policeman stands. Most foreign visitors find such practices amazing at best.

On one trip to Bangkok, I was caught in a

thunderstorm and traffic had virtually ground to a halt. After a long period of time, my companion and I began to become impatient as is natural in such a situation. Just as we were about to complain, our driver suddenly disappeared for twenty minutes. When he returned, we asked where he had gone and he replied that he had gone over to another car to play checkers with the driver, whom he knew.   "This kind of traffic jam will last one to two hours at least,"   he added with a smile.   Needless to say, we had some difficulty finding the immediate humor in the situation.   When the driver learned that we were involved in the electronics business, he asked us to guess what electronics product sells best in Thailand.   "Car stereo. Don't want to be caught in a traffic jam without one!"   he said with a grin.

To me, our driver was the quintessence of the Thai character. Honest, warm, and endearing.   Most importantly, happy and in tune with life, but not necessarily in tune with a logical or legalistic approach to human affairs.

As almost all the Asian countries over the past several hundred years have been occupied by foreign powers, the peoples of such countries have suffered varying degrees of oppression, yet at the same time they have also incorporated systems and values from their occupiers. This exposure has been beneficial in many respects in the course of the society's transformation from an agricultural to an industrial base. Thailand, on the other hand, represents an exception to this rule. As Thailand had never fallen under the control of foreign powers, apart from Bangkok the country remained largely agrarian through the 1980's. From the late 1980's onward, given Thailand's political stability, low-cost labor, and the natural warmth of the people, the wave of foreign capital that washed through Asia came first to Thailand. Investment from Japan was particularly large and was focused on industrial development. (The Japanese preference for Thailand is said to be attributable to similarities in the rice-based diet of both countries, the prevalence of Buddhism in Thailand, and a cultural affinity related to many characteristics of lifestyle).

Unfortunately, Thai society was not prepared for the transformation to an industrial society that the large volumes of foreign investment entailed. The country's legal foundations were underdeveloped, the basic infrastructure was inadequate, attitudes lagged behind the pace of progress, and in the end, not only did the country fail to create a lasting system of wealth creation, even the political foundations of the country came under pressure. Over the past ten years, the country has changed its Prime Minister on average every one or two years.

In addition, Thailand has maintained a traditional over-reliance on the tourist industry. Indeed, tourism accounts for roughly one third of national income. The most successful Thai businessmen have been those that have invested in the property, retail, and leisure industries. Such businessmen took advantage of the investment wave of the 1980s to import foreign capital and borrow overseas. Thus, development efforts in Thailand focused in many cases on areas outside the system of wealth creation. This in turn created a false prosperity in Thailand. Most of the problems which contributed to the region's financial crisis found their roots in Thailand, a country hampered by an uncompetitive export sector, and burdened by over-investment and excessive dependence on foreign capital. Other problems included the failure to establish a wealth-creating system, and emphasis on consumption-related investment, an inability to check the runaway bubble economy, poor financial and banking oversight, and too-aggressive liberalization and internationalization of the capital accounts. The country's open capital accounts allowed in too much short-term foreign capital and destabilized the capital markets. All of these problems combined to ensure that Thailand became the powder keg which set off virtually the entire East Asian economy. As a consequence of these problems, the Thai Baht fell by virtually 50% in value in June 1997 and thus caused a massive contraction in the national wealth. This in turn led to economic depression, collapse in the property and stock markets, and a string of bankruptcies throughout the economy.

Short-term policy response

The first response should be to take necessary measures to erase the trade deficit. These include boosting exports and curbing excessive domestic demand for imported goods. In particular, the government should curb all investment in non wealth-creating areas, while limiting the import of luxury items. The goal should be to achieve a current account surplus, and then to gradually repay debts.

The second response should be to impose appropriate controls on foreign exchange. In the course of conversion from an agrarian to an industrial society, Thailand clearly acted too quickly and failed to make the necessary preparations or take the required precautions. Financial liberalization and internationalization were also introduced too quickly. The best policy response will be to adopt a suitable level of control on foreign exchange and to adopt more conservative fiscal and financial policies.

4.8   Malaysia

Area: 329,749 sq. km.
Population: 21.3m
GDP Per Capita: US$3,930
Exports: US$78.5m
Trade Deficit: US$4.8bn
Foreign Exchange Reserves: US$27.01bn (1996)
External Debt: US$27.1bn

During the 16th Century, foreign traders first arrived in Malaysia. In 1867, England assumed control of the Malay Peninsula and the region first achieved independence in 1957, after which the modern state of Malaysia was created in September, 1963, incorporating Peninsular Malaya, Singapore, Sabah on Northern Borneo, and Sarawak on Northwestern Borneo. In 1965, given tensions between the ethnic Chinese predominant in Singapore and the Malays who controlled Malaysia, Singapore declared independence from Malaysia.

Malaysia consists of peninsular Malaysia and the

northern section of the island of Borneo. The majority of economic activity occurs in peninsular Malaysia. The system of government is based on a constitutional monarchy. The Prime Minister is selected from a council of Sultans (rulers of individual Malaysian states). Administrative control is under the Prime Minister. Mahathir Mohamed has ruled for over ten years and commands a very positive image in Malaysia as a hard-working and caring leader. He is the administrative and spiritual leader of Malaysia and is regarded as sharp and quick-witted. He is also seen as a spokesman for Asian values and is known for his frequent attacks on the US and other western countries.

Current Situation and Problems

The economic policies adopted in 1987 have been extremely successful and allowed the country to achieve the highest per capita income levels in Asia outside Japan and the Dragon economies (around US$4,000). Prior to the East Asian Financial Crisis, many reports suggested that Malaysia be destined to soon become the "Fifth Dragon". Under English rule for over 100 years, Malaysia inherited from

England a set of laws, basic infrastructure, and an industrial society. These, indeed, are perhaps Malaysia's most important assets. Allied to strong political leadership in Malaysia, these assets allowed Malaysia to become perhaps the biggest winner in the investment wave that swept Asia in the 1980's. Those who have visited Malaysia recently are bound to be stunned by the rapid pace of progress achieved in Malaysia. All around can be found the most modern office buildings, department stores, and transportation systems. In addition, civil servants command high respect for their capability and honesty, while the populace is generally very law-abiding. One is especially struck with the confidence of the Malaysian people as they march forward under the banner of the "2020 Vision". The "Great Aspiration" is to become a developed nation.

Up until 1997, Malaysia's growth rate for the recent seven-year period exceeded 8% in each year. Indeed, logic would seem to indicate that Malaysia should not have had an economic crisis at all. Nevertheless, in the latter half of 1997, following the appearance of economic difficulties in neighboring countries such as Thailand, Indonesia, and other countries, the Malaysian Ringgit began to weaken and over a six-month period had fallen by 40%. During that period, Mahathir on several occasions blamed George Soros for speculating on the Asian markets and causing the collapse. The two even exchanged direct verbal fire on one occasion. The strange thing was that on each occasion when Mahathir spoke on the subject, the currency and stock markets dropped in response. This established an almost conditioned response on the part of investors and ensured that a bad situation grew even worse. In the end, Mahathir managed to exercise self-restraint and refrained from public comments on the crisis.

Some have interpreted the financial crisis as it applies to Malaysia as a sort of punishment for Mahathir in response to his past criticisms of Western governments. I personally believe that this type of conspiracy theory is completely without basis and reflects a total lack of understanding over the degree of freedoms of speech and action in the West. In addition, I have found that Westerners generally do not align self-interest with emotion.

While sentiment played a greater role than fundamentals in explaining the drop in the Ringgit, this is not to say that the Malaysian economy was without weaknesses. In the first place, the Malaysian population is relatively small, and this has contributed to a chronic labor shortage and heavy reliance on foreign workers. In addition, labor costs in Malaysia are high, with the average worker earning nearly three times the wages of the average worker in Mainland China. The Malaysian government was well aware of these problems, and thus several years earlier sought to develop a high-tech industrial base in Malaysia. In accompaniment, the government also sought to develop the basic industrial infrastructure, and upgrade basic industry. Unfortunately, the chronic labor shortage and an overly-conservative immigration law, which made it difficult for foreign technicians to remain in the country, contributed to a lack of skilled technicians and engineers. Salaries for technical employees thus skyrocketed and prior to the currency collapses approached level seen in the Dragon economies. Malaysia thus found itself sandwiched between the China and the ASEAN nations below, and the more technologically-proficient Dragon economies above.

In addition, Malaysia also fell victim to over-investment in consumption-related areas and even in infrastructure. Unlike in other Asian economies, this over-investment was not caused by waves of foreign capital but rather by government-led development programs or by domestic groups which funded the projects through overseas borrowings. Thus, as the East Asian Financial Crisis spread and caused economic stagnation, the biggest losers were not foreign investors but rather the Malaysian government and the country's leading corporations.

Short-term policy response

The Malaysian economy is essentially sound. Following the currency depreciation, the export-led economy should see a boost in demand along with widening profitability. This, in turn, should help ease pressure on the current account. In addition, as the Malaysia government has already taken bold steps to reduce consumption expenditures and increase income, the economy should naturally begin to recover gradually in a short period of time.

Despite the generally positive direction for the Malaysian economy, I nonetheless offer two suggestions for the future. The first is to use the funds, experience, confidence and skills accumulated in the public sector over the past ten years of successful economic development and transfer those resources to the private sector, which in some ways has been left behind by rapid public sector development. The government should also give private corporations the chance to lead large-scale development projects.

Another suggestion is that the country should seek more aggressively to attract foreign engineering and technical talent. Given the country's labor shortage and rapid rate of economic growth, Malaysia needs to emulate Taiwan and seek to grow its high-tech sector. Current manpower resources are simply insufficient, however, to allow for successful development of the high-tech sectors. There simply is not enough time either to train the workforce needed to effect the leap into high-tech industry. In addition, high-tech development requires giant steps, as over time the strong tend to become stronger, and the weak weaker. The best solution is to allow foreign technical personnel obtain permanent residency in Malaysia. The current system which permits 5-10 year residency is not adequate to attract the type of high quality talent that Malaysia requires. Nor is 5-10 years sufficient to train a domestic technical workforce. "Technical skill" no longer refers to the ability to repair a car or TV set, skills, which are easily transferable in a relatively short period of time. "Technical skill" at present requires accumulated experience by a large number of skilled workers working together over a long period of time. Such workers must undergo constant training, absorbing a constant stream of state-of-the-art knowledge while striving to conduct related research and development activities on an ongoing basis. This is the only way to achieve a long-term competitive advantage in the high-tech sector.

4.9   Singapore

Area: 646 sq. km.
Population: 3.1m
GDP Per Capita: US$26,400
Exports: US$127.0bn
Trade Surplus: US$14.2bn
Foreign Exchange Reserves: US$76.41bn (1996)
External Debt: nil

Singapore was established in 1819 by the Englishman, Sir Thomas Raffles. Prior to 1959, Singapore was a British colony and the city-state achieved independence from Britain along with Malaysia in September 1963. Upon independence, Singapore was incorporated as a State in the Malaysian Republic.

Owing to political tensions between the Malays who ruled Malaysia and the Chinese who dominated in Singapore, Singapore and Malaysia reached an agreement in August 1965 to allow Singapore to become an independent republic.

Singapore is located on a small island at the southern tip of the Malay Peninsula. The island covers only around 600 sq. km, or roughly twice the size of Taipei City. Of the population of 3m, ethnic Chinese account for roughly 80%. Thirty years ago, at the time of independence, Singapore was a poor island city-state. Under the decisive leadership of former Prime Minister Mr. Lee Kwan-yew, however, the tiny island created an economic miracle. By 1996, Singapore formally qualified as a developed nation. Those who visit Singapore are amazed to find that this Chinese administered island paradise boasts a beautiful and clean environment, orderly traffic, and a law-abiding populace that lives a healthy lifestyle. To describe Singapore as the "Switzerland of the Orient" is in no sense an exaggeration.

Current Situation and Problems

Aside from clean government and inspired leadership, two other key factors have allowed the postage-stamp sized city state of Singapore to thrive. The first is that the island successfully became the "Operating Center" for Southeast Asia. Indeed, taking advantage of its location between Malaysia and

Indonesia, just as the latter two countries followed a development strategy focused on the export of raw materials, resource-poor Singapore had no choice but to make use of its geographic position to establish itself as a center for transshipment, trading, finance, education, and other types of services. To facilitate this transformation, Singapore built an enviably complete infrastructure, made English the national language, created a safe and peaceful living environment, and developed an excellent education system. All these attributes helped Singapore encourage multinational corporations to establish their regional headquarters in Singapore or even transfer their headquarters to Singapore from other locations.

The other highly successful development policy which Singapore employed was to attract direct investment from multinational corporations. To do so, the government established the appropriate legal environment and also offered tax incentives. The government, furthermore, created an environment in which expatriates preferred to live and trained a workforce suited to employment in multinational corporations. Having put the basics in place, the Singapore government then traveled the world over to attract multinational direct investment.

In its programs, the government spared no efforts. To attract Japanese investment, for instance, the government not only established a Japanese school and attracted Japanese department stores and restaurants to the island, the government also ensured there were Japanese bookstores and Japanese-style entertainment venues. Currently there are roughly 30,000 Japanese living in Singapore, representing approximately 1% of the population.

Transshipment, triangular trade, and the trading activities of the large multinational corporations operating in Singapore have allowed this island of just 3m to tally exports of over US$100bn, roughly in line with Taiwan. Per Capita Income is also second highest in Asia, behind only Japan.

Many commentators have indicated that the government in its headlong rush to develop Singapore, has made the island into a corporation, Singapore Inc.. If indeed this is the case, then it is fair to say that Singapore is the world's largest corporation, and probably also its most efficient and most profitable.

While Singapore has been very successful, the story has its pitfalls as well. Over the past ten years, neighboring Malaysia has sought to emulate Singapore's success, especially in the area of attracting foreign multinational investment. Malaysia's policies in this regard seem to have been copied straight from Singapore's book. In addition, Malaysian wages are only one third as high as those are in Singapore, thus many foreign multinational corporations have been willing to make the switch from Malaysia to Singapore.

Because domestic labor costs are high in Singapore, and because land resources are limited, Singapore has developed a policy of "expanding beyond its borders". On nearby Batan Island (an Indonesian island of 450 sq. km., or roughly four thirds the size of Singapore) just a 20 minute boatride away from Singapore, Singapore has cooperated with Indonesia to develop a manufacturing center. In addition, Singapore has also cooperated with the PRC government to construct an industrial park near Suzhou (roughly 70 sq. km.) The idea is to use the Singapore system of management, while taking advantage of the low cost land and labor to recreate the Singapore miracle and attract foreign investment.

At present, it is too early to determine the success

of these plans. If they are successful, and can be repeated in other locations, then this will bring economic blessing not only to Singapore, but also to other developing countries.

As a result of the East Asian Financial Crisis the Singapore Dollar has fallen by approximately 20%. Given Singapore's sound operating base and large accumulation of foreign currency reserves, the short-term impact of the crisis should scarcely make a dent in the island's economy. Over the mid- and longer-term, however, the crisis still may pose a threat to Singapore's economic success. Firstly, the prime reason for Singapore's economic success - the fact that is a regional operations center - is jeopardized simply because of economic stagnation in neighboring countries. In addition, in attracting foreign direct investment, (the second reason for Singapore's economic success) the depreciation of the neighboring Malaysia's Ringgit will add to competitive pressures on Singapore.

Of course, it is difficult to distill an analysis of Singapore's highly-successful economy into such a narrow framework. In this analysis, we approach the problem only in the broadest terms, with an aim to introduce Singapore's basic current economic situation and potential economic problems.

Short-term policy response

Having already achieved the second highest per capita income in Asia next to Japan, it will not be easy for resource-poor Singapore to continue its economic success using the policies of the past. This, despite Singapore's high efficiency and complete infrastructure, the imperative is to create a new strategy for growth. These can include expanding beyond its borders, becoming a computer networking center, and other innovative approaches to development. I am sure that the far-sighted Singapore government, experienced as is it in international affairs, likely already has the answer to these pressing questions.

4.10   Indonesia

Area: 1.91m sq. km.
Population: 200m
GDP Per Capita: US$1,086
Exports: US$53.6bn
Trade Deficit: US$8.9bn
Foreign Exchange Reserves: US$18.25bn (1996)
External Debt: US$137.4bn

Approximately two thousand years ago, Hindu and Buddhist civilization reached the shores of Indonesia, especially on the island of Java. During the 15th Century, Muslim traders came to Indonesia, and by the 16th Century had become the main source of economic energy in the region. During the 17th Century, the Dutch replaced the Portuguese to become the region's largest trading partner. By 1750, the Dutch had already gained control of Java, and by the 20th Century were already in control of the entire Indonesian Island chain.

From 1942 to 1945, Japan occupied Indonesia

and by the end of the Second World War, Sukarno had already announced the formation of a Republic. After a four-year sporadic guerilla campaign, the Dutch in December, 1949 eventually recognized Indonesia's independence, but the Dutch retained control over New Guinea and West Irian Jaya.

In 1957, the Dutch rejected Indonesian demands for control over West Irian Jaya, causing an international dispute. By 1963, the U.N. had adopted a resolution calling for the Dutch to transfer West Irian Jaya to Indonesia. In 1969, a public referendum in West Irian Jaya approved annexation by Indonesia.

In the course of the East Asian Financial Crisis, the Indonesian currency, the Rupiah, experienced the largest decline in value of any Asian currency, having dropped by as much as 70% to 80%. Even at present, the currency continues to exhibit extreme volatility. In thinking about Indonesia, many immediately conjure up an image of a multitudinous, poor, corrupt, anti-Chinese society. This image is enhanced by a series of recent negative media reports which have reinforced Indonesia's poor international image.

The reality, however, is somewhat different. Indonesia has been independent for fewer than 50 years. For a nation of 200m spread over more than 10,000 islands and led by a government relatively inexperienced in international affairs to rise within a ten-year period to command a national income of over US$1,000 is not an easy task. Indeed, when compared with many of the poorer nations of Indochina (such as Vietnam and Burma) and many Southwest Asian nations, the success of the Indonesian government over the past ten years is particularly impressive. In visiting Indonesia, one is also impressed with the assiduousness of the Indonesian worker, as well as the zest for life that characterizes the typical Indonesian.

Current Situation and Problems

Over the past 32 years, Indonesia had been under the autocratic rule of military strongman Suharto. The Suharto family and its cohorts took control of all levers of power in the island nation. Economic control rested also in the hands of just ten or more large corporations run by Indonesian Chinese. As these two forces came together, it was easy for Indonesia to rapidly exploit and develop its natural resources to create wealth. Indeed, this was the Indonesian model for growth over a short period of several decades.

It is not fair to take a one-sided view that this form of development strategy entails a too-cosy relationship between the government and business sector. For a country that had just shaken off the shackles of colonialism, ruled by a government with relatively little experience in governance, and under the pressure of needing to feed an impoverished population of 200m, such a development strategy was in many ways a necessity.

Thus, a strong government worked hand-in-hand with an efficient Chinese-led business community to exploit Indonesia's natural resources and create wealth for the nation. This model of development provided for several decades of economic growth, but also sowed the seeds of economic weakness. Firstly, authoritarian regimes almost always become corrupt. In addition, after thirty two years in power, Suharto had already become 76 years old, and his Indonesian Chinese business cronies were also in their 70's and 80's. Political and corporate aging, combined with a global trend away from resource development in favor of knowledge development meant that resource-rich Indonesia gradually lost its economic strength.

As a result of the East Asian Financial Crisis, Indonesia's rampant corruption and problem of aging came to the fore. Authorities also found it difficult to control the emotions of Indonesia's huge population once the currency began to slip. The populace thus quickly lost confidence in the currency, and led to the economic collapse which eventually brought down the Suharto regime.

Indeed, the annals of history are strewn with examples of economic problems leading to social problems and even political instability. Thus the Chinese expression "lean times breed bandits". It was not surprising then that Indonesia's economic problems quickly became social problems (including attacks on Chinese-owned businesses) and then eventually the political problems that brought down the Suharto regime.

Short-term policy response

The first response must be to stabilize the political situation and restore order. If economic chaos persists, then political instability is surely not far behind. In the same way, the economy cannot grow as long as political instability and social disorder persist.

The second response must be to develop a long-term economic development strategy. Cosy cooperation between the public and private sectors that worked so well in the distant past and an emphasis on resource-based development are no longer viable policies in the current era. The government must seek to create a new basis for economic growth, including inviting in foreign companies to assist in development of Indonesia's natural resources, and opening of Indonesian islands to development by foreign companies or even countries (such as Singapore). Such bold measures may be the medicine needed to help pull Indonesia out of its current dire economic straits.

4.11 Vietnam, Laos, Cambodia, Myanmar

Of the 500m people of Southeast Asia we typically think of the fast growing nations of ASEAN and often forget about the 100m impoverished "orphans of Asia" living mainly along the banks of the Mekong River in Vietnam, Laos, Cambodia, and Myanmar. This is the so-called "Mekong Delta" region.

Vietnam:

Population: 77.8m
GDP Per Capita: US$270
Exports: US$8bn
Trade Deficit: US$2.9bn
External Debt: US$26.5bn

The Vietnamese trace their roots back to central China and prior to 939 A.D. Vietnam had consistently been incorporated as a part of China. Even after later achieving a measure of independence, Vietnam was still often a protectorate or tributary of China. In 1288,

Vietnam achieved independence after beating back the
Mongol Invaders of the Yuan Dynasty, but in 1858 the
nation fell under the control of the French and became
a French colony.

After the conclusion of World War II, the French-
controlled South and the communist-occupied North
became embroiled in a lengthy conflict. In 1954, a
cease-fire was arranged and the French pulled out of
South, leaving the 17th parallel as the border between
the two Vietnams.

Following the French pullout, however, the conflict
between North and South Vietnam continued and by
1959, the conflict had escalated. In that year, the
South accepted assistance from the US, while the
North turned to China. The war continued from that
time until 1973 when the Paris Peace accords provided
for a US pullout. North Vietnam violated the accords,
however, and continued large-scale attacks on South
Vietnam. In April, 1975, South Vietnam fell to the
North and Vietnam was unified.

Laos

Population: 5m
GDP Per Capita: US$370
Exports: US$300m
Trade Deficit: US$300m
External Debt: US$2.2bn

Laos became a French colony in 1893 and won independence in 1949 as a constitutional monarchy. Conflict between the conservative ruling faction and the Laotian Communist party ran unabated. Finally, in 1960 open conflict broke out between the Communist party under the leadership of Prince Souvannarath and the ruling Royal family and its supporters in the Laotian Army. In 1962, a coalition government was established, with the neutral Prince Phouma as Premier. At the time, Laos signed accords in Geneva guaranteeing the country's neutrality. In 1964, however, the communists pulled out of the ruling coalition, sparking renewed fighting, and in December, 1975 the communists won control of the government and established the People's Republic of Laos.

Cambodia

Population: 10.3m
GDP Per Capita: US$270
Exports: US$600m
Trade Deficit: US$300m
External Debt: US$2bn

In the first century A.D., present-day Cambodia fell under the control of the Khmer Kingdom. The kingdom reached its zenith in the 9th Century and began to decline in the 13th Century. The region became a French colony in 1863, but became a kingdom in 1947 before finally winning independence from France in 1953.

From 1941 to 1955, Prince Norodom Sihanouk reigned as ruler of the region. In 1960, his title was transferred to that of Premier and he sought strenuously to maintain Cambodia's neutrality as war raged throughout Indochina. In 1970, pro-US strongman Lon Nol gained power and ended the monarchy while creating the Republic of Cambodia. In

1975, the army under Lon Nol was defeated by the Khmer Rouge communist insurgency. The Khmer Rouge, in turn, was pushed from power in 1979 following infiltration from Vietnam by the pro-Vietnamese Kampuchean People's Salvation Front. On gaining power, the Front established a new government with Hun Sen at its head.

Myanmar

Population: 48.8m
GDP Per Capita: US$765
Exports: US$1bn
Trade Deficit: US$300m
External Debt: US$5.3bn

In the 9th Century A.D. Myanmar was settled by people's emigrating from present-day Tibet. By the 10th Century these peoples had established a Buddhist Kingdom in Myanmar. In 1272, Yuan Dynasty Mongol invaders captured Myanmar, and Myanmar remained a part of China until the 16th Century.

From 1824 to 1884, Myanmar remained under British control and was administered as a part of India. By 1937, Myanmar had achieved self-rule, but fell under Japanese occupation during WWII and only achieved independence after the war. From 1958 until the present, Myanmar has remained under the control of General Ne Win. In 1962, Ne Win established a ruling junta and sought to implement socialist economic policies.

Thailand sits as the hub of all the Indochinese economies. Most of these economies have instituted tight capital controls and are mired in poverty. As a result, these economies have mainly escaped the ravages of the East Asian Financial Crisis. Nevertheless, because these economies are reliant on the ASEAN economies, they are likely to also suffer long-lasting effects from the crisis on a par with the ASEAN economies. Metaphorically, it is as if a poor person lived next to a millionaire and subsisted by performing small tasks for the millionaire. One day, the millionaire is robbed of his wealth and is forced to cut down on expenses. Although the poor person himself was not robbed, his financial situation is likely to suffer perhaps to an even greater extent than that of the millionaire.

In August, 1996, I went with a friend to Ho Chih Minh City (the former Saigon), my previous visit having been in 1974 at the tail end of the Vietnam War. It is worth noting that the fighting was actually at its most bitter in those last few months of the war, and three or four months after my visit, Saigon fell to the

Communists and Vietnam was united under Ho Chih Minh. At night I slept in a deserted hotel and off in the distance I could hear the sound of exploding artillery and see flashes of light in the nighttime sky. Upon my return 22 years later, I was moved to see Saigon after such a long absence. My companion was even more moved, for he was an Overseas Chinese who grew up in Saigon and came to Taiwan to study in University. Following a period of studies in the US, he had last seen his home in Vietnam only 31 years earlier.

What surprised us most was that even though there had been a wave of foreign interest and investment in Vietnam, and even though Saigon was the most developed and prosperous of the cities in the Mekong Delta. It appeared to us that the city had changed little over the twenty or thirty years since we had last visited. Aside from a few cosmetic changes and a few new hotels, much remained just as it had been. Indeed, many of the homes and shops near my friend's old house were worse off than they had been thirty years earlier. This is similar to the experience an overseas Chinese friend related when he visited his old home in Rangoon after an absence of 30 years. He said it was as if "history had just stopped".

On my third day in Saigon, we went to visit the past residence, office, and air raid shelter of former South Vietnamese President Nguyen Van Thieu. It happened that at this time Pepsi Cola was in the middle of a marketing promotion, and all around were red, white and blue balloons, gorgeous models, new wave music, and throngs of spectators. I thought back to that period 22 years earlier and could almost hear the thunder of cannon fire and could almost recall the nightly TV images of wounded South Vietnamese and US soldiers. Suddenly, I was overcome by a strong sense that history had become disjointed. History teaches us that owing to lack of wisdom or patience, mankind creates tragedy, and it is usually the innocent that suffer most in the course of such tragedy. I wondered if there were any parallels to the current East Asian Financial Crisis to be drawn from this analogy.

On my fourth day in Saigon, I not only went sightseeing, I also went to visit local government officials and business leaders. I also went to visit several industrial parks. On this day, I not only developed a greater appreciation for the wounds that Vietnam had suffered, I also was greatly moved to see how intent the Taiwanese businessmen in Saigon were on creating a success of their investment in Vietnam.

Indeed, the Taiwanese in Vietnam were in a difficult environment in every sense of the word. Most of the countries of the Mekong Delta lack the basic legal infrastructure necessary for promoting industrial development. Even basic rules of business conduct are lacking. In addition, living standards are low, and the nations of the Delta generally lack the basic luxuries to which most of us have become accustomed. Foreign investors for the most part have been reluctant to invest in the region, but Taiwanese investors have moved in aggressively to fill the void. Even in remote jungle areas, Taiwanese have established industrial parks. Countless Taiwanese have left their homes and family to work side-by-side with local employees and build viable businesses. It is not uncommon to find the Taiwanese factory owners eating and sleeping under the same roof with the factory employees.

While I myself am a Taiwanese businessman, I was nevertheless struck by a newfound appreciation for the pioneering spirit of the Taiwanese entrepreneurs who dauntlessly invest throughout Asia.

They come from a land of uncertain international standing, and taking with them only money and skill, go off to invest in regions that lack even the most basic investment protections. They can be found everywhere throughout Southeast Asia, from the large cities to the most remote villages. Fearing neither poverty nor hardship, in many cases risking even their lives, they tireless work to build businesses and in the process also bring badly-needed tangible benefits to the communities in which they invest. Often in their work they are misunderstood even by their own countrymen and families. When I think of this point in particular, it often brings tears to my eyes. Whether these entrepreneurs work for fortune, fame, or in pursuit of some distant ideal, they give their all while fulfilling the responsibility to play a positive role in the East Asian community. Perhaps most importantly, they bring a ray of light to throngs of people mired in poverty and hopelessness.

4.12 Personal Financial Management Strategies and the East Asian Financial Crisis

Whenever the subject of the East Asian Financial Crisis arises, the question of how to manage one's personal wealth usually follows shortly thereafter. In this respect, we must be honest with ourselves, for against the mammoth forces at work in the regional economy, the average East Asian feels utterly helpless and rightly so. Options for managing personal wealth in the face of the crisis are therefore limited.

In my book *Success with Money & Joy*, I stressed the importance of personal financial management, and at this time I would like to take the opportunity to stress again the idea that those who do not learn to manage their personal finances are doomed to a life of poverty. It is especially important that young people just entering society remember the importance of personal financial management.

A.   *Wealth must be Persisent and Consistent*
Many people go through their entire lives without appreciating the idea that wealth must be persistent and consistent. In our modern, industrialised society,

we require money at nearly every minute of the day, but we sometimes fail to realize that we can't earn money just any time we feel like doing so. Many people feel that if they "have enough to get by", that this is a sufficient basis for managing personal wealth. I disagree. "Enough to get by" is not enough. A building whose pipes are filled with water does not have enough water for the inhabitants to "have enough". A storage tank filled with water is necessary before the building has "enough water". Rather than just trying to "get by", people should strive to be well off, and to maintain wealth on a consistent basis. Once one accumulates a nest egg, one shouldn't start to carelessly spend one's wealth or lend it to others. The first step in personal financial management is to make sure that one's own bank account or pockets are consistently filled with money.

B.   Concepts Relating to Modern Financial Structure

In an agrarian society, land is the most important store of wealth. In our modern industrial society, the frequency of financial transactions has multiplied exponentially and money has replaced land as the most important medium for storage of wealth. In the past, money was typically created from gold or other precious metals. Today, money is issued by the nation's central bank. The average citizen works hard to earn the money issued by his government, spends what he needs on daily necessities, and places the remainder in a savings deposit where it earns interest and grows to an amount large enough to allow the citizen to buy a car, house or other "large ticket" items. At times, perhaps, the citizen may use a little of his money to invest in the stock market.

With respect to the structure of savings in the modern era, we can identify four broad categories for saving or investment. These include tangible assets, real estate, marketable securities, and money. Typically, one's personal savings are spread among these four categories with adjustments made from time to time. Less liquid items such as property or buildings are referred to as real estate. More liquid items such as cars or gold are referred to as tangible assets, while stocks, bonds, and mutual funds are all marketable securities, and cash is the most common type of money.

The typical Westerner generally knows how best

to divide his personal assets among the four categories listed above. He allocates his wealth among the four categories with an eye to protecting the value of his assets while also seeking the highest return. East Asians, on the other hand, have typically held onto superstitions concerning the importance of owning real estate or cars or other types of assets which may or may not be the best choice for a given individual. Following the East Asian Financial Crisis, it is critical that East Asians develop a more modern and more scientific approach to structuring their personal wealth.

The least wealthy were probably hurt most badly as a result of the East Asian Financial Crisis. The winners are those that seek always to be "well off", those that diversify their savings across the four broad categories of financial assets, and those that continually search for increased knowledge and information concerning all types of financial products. Let us all learn to manage our money well in the new era ushered in by the East Asian Financial Crisis.

Having discussed the causes and effects of the crisis in East Asia, we now outline what we feel to be the best course of action for the future.

5. Long-term Policy Response

After the impact of civilization's transformation, we have to rapidly adjust to a new computer and communication *(C&C)* lifestyle, whether we like it or not.

Just as modern medicine is still unable to cure many types of disease, with hope still held out for some future cure, so might even the most insurmountable economic problems one day be solved. In the same way, it is difficult to spell out a proper "treatment" for East Asia in the aftermath of the crisis, because the solution to Asia's problems lies in a world yet to come. Nevertheless, we outline a few measures which can be used to help cure the region's financial ills and pave the way to a brighter tomorrow.

5.1   Establish Wealth-crediting Systems

When a country invites in foreign investment, it does so on the basis of the value of the investment or in order to enjoy the reputational benefits of having a renowned company invest in the country. In meeting these requirements, however, the host country's time and resources are often mis-allocated. Even the most advanced countries like the US, Japan and those in Western Europe aren't able to specialize in every industry. They specialize in the areas where they have competitive advantage and buy what they do not have competitive advantage in. That's why there's international trade. Introducing foreign investment without a blueprint can be a very dangerous strategy. As the host country has limited control over foreign investments it receives, there is little the host country can do if the foreign investor decides one day to leave the country. Not only will the local economy potentially suffer from the closure of the foreign business but local investments and skills related to supporting the foreign investment may be wasted.

Some western economists recently questioned whether the East Asia 'miracle' was in fact merely a bubble. Their point was that rapid economic growth came mainly on the back of cheap labour and not innovation and, therefore, may have been limited in its scope and potential. While this may not be completely true, it is nonetheless a good starting point for a re-examination of investment strategy in the region.

Each country or region has the capacity to produce some goods and services better than others do and it is incumbent on that country to discover where its niche lies so that it can develop a competitive edge in the long term. On the one hand, the host country should encourage foreign and local investment in its chosen niches while on the other hand, it should nurture local companies to become involved in supporting industries. Prime examples of this niche marketing approach are the development of the shoe industry in Italy or of the watch-making industry in Switzerland. Both of these industries should continue to be strong foreign currency earners for their respective countries in the long-term.

Just as a man with a good skill will always be able to take care of himself so is it the same for countries and regions. A country with its own wealth-creating activities is less likely to be caught up in financial troubles that sweep its shores. Of course, the development of a sustainable competitive advantage requires time and may take anything from five to twenty years but it must be emphasised that no long-term economic development strategy is viable unless a country develops wealth-creating activities of its own.

5.2 Solidify Financial Oversight and Establish a Financial Defense System

When a company runs low on cash, it only needs one or two reliable financial professionals to handle the situation satisfactorily. As the company expands, however, and the volume of external transactions multiplies, the company requires a transparent and reliable system for financial management. Indeed, the company must also computerize. A nation's financial system is responsible for managing the nation's public and private sector wealth, and the speed and complexity of transactions at the national level is in no way slower than that at the level of individual companies. Therefore, a successful national financial management system must include a number of key characteristics.

A. *Transparency and Structure*

A nation's financial system is the pillar of support for the national wealth. It can no longer be operated as a black box by a few elite specialists. It must be transparent and well-structured. In this respect, the financial systems of the Western nations have been successful for several decades. East Asian nations would do well to copy these systems and make adjustments where national characteristics necessitate.

B. *Computerization*

In today's world, money travels around the globe at the speed of light. Banks which transmit funds or react to financial developments too slowly will eventually lose competitiveness and will be driven out of the market. The only way to stay on top of the ever-changing global marketplace is to embark on a continual program of computerization. In the past, computerization in a bank tended to be limited to a small information technology unit. From this point onward, computerization must be pushed throughout all levels of the organization, including the top management.

C. *Training of Financial Management Personnel*

Having visited many banks in the East Asian Region, at times I have been amazed to find that the equipment which many banks use are outdated, and high-quality manpower resources are often inadequate, especially when compared with staffing levels at major international banks or even local industrial firms. Without proper equipment and adequately trained staff, there is virtually no way to successfully run a modern bank. This is especially true in the present age of international competition.

From this standpoint, it is no wonder that when the East Asian Financial Crisis broke, so many banks in the region were woefully unprepared. If banks throughout the region are to enhance their competitiveness, they will need to tear down overly-conservative personnel management systems and must seek to rely on a younger workforce supported by better training systems.

D. Construct a Financial Defense System

When a foreigner wishes to cross a country's borders, he often needs a visa. If he seeks to sneak across the border, he is likely to face serious obstacles. If a foreign army prepares to invade a neighboring country and steal that country's national resources, the country threatened will most certainly have a national defense system in place established to block outside invaders. Most East Asian countries place strong emphasis on national defense and military preparedness. Some countries in the region, in fact, continue to be led my military strongmen.

When a country's financial markets are opened, liberalized, and linked to the outside world, then international investors and speculators may be free to enter and conduct financial transactions. In an instant, speculators may be able to make off with vast amounts of a country's wealth. Just as nations maintain customs bureaus, and immigration police, so should they also have systems in place to protect national wealth in the event that foreigners launch a speculative attack on the nation's financial system. In the world of the future, it may not be military strongmen, but rather financial "strongmen" who hold the reins to power in many countries.

The development of a sound national financial management and financial defense system must be a top policy priority for every country. The passage of one or two laws is not enough to ensure a nation's financial security. What is required in the region is a determined effort at top-down financial reform. This reform includes the import of systems from the advanced western nations, wide-scale computerization, and training of high-quality and internationalized financial specialists. To be effective, such reform must unfold as a continuous process carried out in perpetuity.

5.3 Develop "Computer and Communications" (C&C) Industries

In January of 1978, when Bill Gates was still just 23 years old, the Consumer Electronics Show held in Las Vegas of that year was filled with products from Japan, Korea, Taiwan, Hong Kong and other areas. The products included TVs, VCRs, stereos, calculators, electronic clocks, and other products. At that time, the US electronics industry appeared to be on the verge of fading away. Many commentators whispered sarcastically that the oldest and largest electronics show in the US could now be transformed into an import exhibition. Little did I or anyone else know that just at the time when I was attending that Las Vegas Electronics Show, an event of enormous import for the world economy was quietly underway.

Normally, at an electronics show, the exhibitors set up booths to display their latest products in hopes of attracting buyers. Seminars, however, are also an important feature of such shows. The organizing committee typically invites a variety of industry experts to speak on the various products or technologies on exhibit at the show. Usually such speeches or seminars are also followed by a question-and-answer session.

I remember that on the last day of the exhibition, when most of the participants had already begun to dismantle their booths and many participants had already left the exhibit hall, the organizing committee made a last minute change to the conference schedule and changed the seminar on "Calculators and Watches" to one on "Personal Computers". Prior to that time, the term "Personal Computer" had never been used.

I still remember that the five seminar panelists for that seminar were from Apple Computer, Radio Shack, Commodore, APF and Video Brain. (Aside from Apple Computer, none of the other companies are still active in the computer industry). Most in attendance at the meeting were drawn in by curiosity and a healthy dose of skepticism over this strange new product called a "Personal Computer"

The three or four years following that seminar were a period of constant strife in the industry. Hundreds of companies sprang up touting their products. Of these, Apple Computer gradually became recognized as a leader.

Apple Computer was founded by a 20 year-old college drop out named Steve Jobs. He built his own computer at home, and virtually sold it door-to-door. While he lacked funding and experience, he was a computer whiz, and in the open and free marketplace of America, was able to build his own computer empire.

In 1981, IBM finally began to pay attention to the burgeoning market for personal computers. Long focused on mainframe models, IBM in the past had underestimated the importance of the mini-computer and had conceded large portions of this market to Digital, Wang and others. Thus, with the emergence of the PC market, IBM realized that it could not afford to make the same mistake again.

As the PC market was small, however, IBM decided not to devote a great deal of internal resources to the market. Instead, it opted to use Intel microprocessors and an operating system supplied by Microsoft.

Typically, most computer companies sought to control the technology for the CPU and the operating system. At this time, however, IBM made a conscious decision to use technologies supplied by outside vendors. IBM even allowed Intel and Microsoft to supply their products to other computer companies, in effect creating a new industry standard aimed at eroding Apple's industry dominance. Given IBM's global marketing strength, the IBM standard quickly became a global industry standard. From 1982 onward, a number of new entrants joined the market place, including Compaq, Dell, Acer and others.

The IBM PC standard fostered an entire new industry, and created a whole new breed of wealthy technocrats, while at the same time restraining Apple's growth. Perhaps most importantly, these developments created two new giants, Intel and Microsoft.

Intel previously had been a mid-sized semiconductor company. Under the far-sighted leadership of Chairman Andy Grove, it grasped the opportunity to supply CPUs to IBM and introduced a series of compatible CPU products from the 8088, to 80286, 80386, 80486, to Pentium. The CPU is, of course, the engine of the computer. It controls the computer's ability to make calculations and as of 1996, Intel had become the largest semiconductor producer in the world as well as the world's most profitable electronics manufacturer.

Microsoft's founder, Bill Gates, is another college dropout who also happened to be a computer whiz. The developments he engineered in the software industry and his business achievements in no way pale by comparison with Andy Grove. In fact, Intel and Microsoft have a long history of close cooperation, and through such cooperation, the two companies not only helped create a whole new class of PC products, they also helped to attract to the industry large numbers of hardware providers, including those from East Asia. The end result was to create history's largest industry, the modern electronics industry. Building Microsoft up from a small start-up, Bill Gates managed in a short ten-year period to become the youngest person ever to become the world's richest man. In the US and around the world he is looked up to by many as a modern day hero.

The PC industry, with Intel, Microsoft, and Compaq at its fore (and with many Taiwanese companies also playing a vital role) quickly combined with the communications industry and gobbled up the office automation market, displacing such dinosaurs as the word processor and facsimile machine. At the same time, the PC industry took huge swathes of market share away from the mini-computer industry and forced companies such as Digital, Wang and others either into mergers or liquidation. At the same time, the merger of computing and communications, coupled with the advent of the Internet, has already begun to threaten the foundations of the mainframe market.

Indeed, the Computer and Communications industries are already the world's largest industries, and most importantly, are the world's fastest growing industries. In a world where most industries are beset with over supply, the Computer and Communications industry continues to shine, largely because it continues to be characterized by constant innovation.

While today's Computer and Communications industry has already overtaken the traditional three large industries (Automotives, Steel, and Petrochemicals), global penetration rates for computers and cellular phones remain below 5%. Clearly this is a market with huge future potential.

Although many East Asian countries retain a cautious attitude towards the fast-moving and technology-intensive Computer and Communications

Industry, the waves of change are irreversible. I would assert that it is better to be a bit player in a fast growing industry, than a leader in an industry beset by oversupply and stagnation. It pays to remember as well that the Computer and Communications industry is already spelling the demise of many older, traditional industries.

5.4 Foster a C&C Environment

An Officeless Person

From August, 1992 to the present, I have attempted to become officeless. Over the past five years, whether on business or vacation, I have travelled only with a notebook PC, cellular phone and electronic dictionary/organizer. In any given year, I might spend up to 300 days in a hotel room in one city or another. Using only the hotel's phone line, I can read reports daily from offices in my company the world over, and can respond by phone or E-Mail.

I continually challenge my own concepts of the proper "office". Over the past five years, I have found that I have not had any significant difficulties at all in making the adjustment to "officelessness". On the contrary, by becoming "officeless", I find that the time available for me to add value to the organization increases. I have found that my productivity has increased, and at the same time I have learned many of the secrets of the "officeless company" heralded by many as the wave of the future.

Over the short term, I concede it will not be easy to liberate the majority from their offices. Nevertheless, using today's technology, it is possible for corporations to create "virtual offices".

A company with 1,000 employees may not need to concentrate all its employees in the mid-town office. Perhaps the office can be divided into 5 or 6 smaller offices linked by a computer and communications network. In this way, the marketing department can be located near the highest concentration of customers, the purchasing department near the company's suppliers, the financial department near banks, and the R&D department in a quieter location. In this way, a company can not only reduce the time needed to commute to and from work, but it can also reduce the cost of office rentals and employee housing.

Futurist Alvin Toffler, in his work *The Third Wave*, once predicted that "within our lifetimes, we may witness empty cities, just as one hundred year earlier our ancestors couldn't imagine why anyone would leave the countryside to live in a high-rise apartment in the big city."

Make the Most of Computing and Communication Equipment

If a country wishes to develop its computing and communications (C&C) industries, it generally must possess a minimum set of accompanying conditions, and such conditions are not always easily met. However, any country can invest in C&C equipment to replace the traditional investments in consumption-related industries. With respect to the amount of value that today's C&C equipment can create in a society, the price of such equipment is extremely low. If developing countries wish to continue to grow, they must not only invest in skyscrapers, department stores, highways, and other large-scale projects, they must also carefully invest in a C&C backbone to create the high-speed information networks so critical to the development of a cost-competitive information society.

The rapid introduction of C&C equipment into an economy can help to create a broadbased C&C

environment. If we are willing to open our markets to foreign fast food chains, department stores, or clothing boutiques, why not open our market to foreign C&C equipment as well! East Asia is one of the major global production centres for computer and communications systems and equipment but the installation rate in the region is relatively low. The opening up of the region's 2bn-strong market to these products will not only help bring East Asian countries into the information society sooner but will also offer an outlet for producers around the world and in the region.

5.5 Promote C&C Lifestyles

The most important form of evening entertainment in Japan is to sing Karaoke. Karaoke and KTV's can be found in large cities and small towns across the entire nation. In fact, the industry is enormous in terms of value and continues to grow. The Japanese in 1997 were surprised to find that the Karaoke/KTV industry actually registered a decline, however, with receipts falling by 10%. The industry association thus performed a survey to discover why receipts had fallen. Surprisingly, the results showed that the decline was due to an increase in popularity of the PHS (similar in function to a cellular phone but with significantly lower phone rates). Because the price of the PHS had fallen, 20% of high school and college students has purchased PHS units and thus could easily contact classmates and friends. Unfortunately for Karaoke/KTV operators, these young people spent a considerable portion of their disposable income on phonecalls, rather than singing songs at KTVs or Karaokes.

From this example, it is readily apparent that new technologies can have a significant affect on existing traditional industries. This, however, is only the tip of the iceberg. Indeed, the widespread use of computing, communication and networking technologies has opened the door to a new "information society" which will continue to alter our basic lifestyles. As we have discussed, the East Asian Financial Crisis was caused in large part because revolutionary new C&C technology has allowed for the creation of more rapid global financial networks. The introduction of such technology represents a turning point in human history and is an historical inevitability.

Whether we like it or not, the moment we open the door to international trade and connect to global financial networks, we (and our financial assets) are surrounded, pushed and pulled by the information current that swirls daily around the globe. I am quite sure that this current will impact the global economy in a far greater way than even the industrial revolution. Fortunately, technological change also makes entry into the information age much cheaper than was the case during the transition between the agriculture-based and industrial societies of the last century. In today's case, all that needs to be adjusted is the mind-set of economic players, for any government that is clean, efficient, and interferes little can bring about such a technological revolution.

A lifestyle based on the C&C revolution is bound to be more rational and more fulfilling than that which we enjoy now. It is a near certainty that many currently unimaginable technologies will spring from the ongoing C&C revolution and will completely change the way mankind lives, works and plays.

In the aftermath of the East Asian Financial Crisis,

I am confident that the new society we create will be a better one and will differ from the last in many ways. The following are two examples which will hopefully help those still shell-shocked by the recent financial troubles to see the way forward.

Electronic Money

Money is a medium of exchange and a store of value. It has taken the form of metal, paper and most recently, plastic. In the IT age, however, money will be in the form of electronic signals, which can travel at high speeds. When we pay our bill by credit card, the electronic signal flows from the card reader to the card center, is acknowledged and then flows back to the printer where a slip is printed. The process is completed in only a few seconds. In the future, savings may not even be in one currency only, for smart credit cards can allow us to choose the most advantageous currency in which to pay.

Smart Bank

After the recent economic crisis, a lot of people may transfer their savings into banks with better credit. Weaker or poorly managed banks may be closed down or bought out. Even those that survive will meet with new challenges in the future. Banks of the future will not merely provide savings, loans and interest, they will also protect the value of clients' savings and offer a whole new array of services.

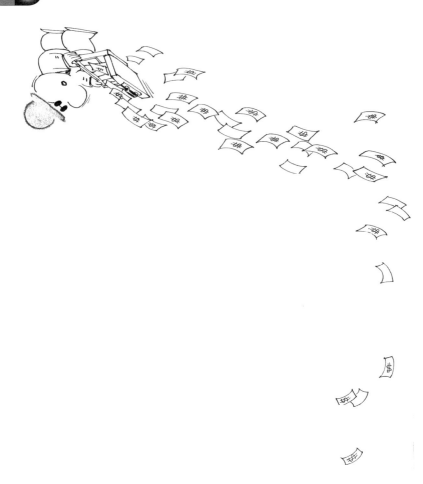

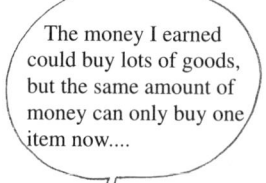

The money I earned could buy lots of goods, but the same amount of money can only buy one item now....

It's because the money you make is soft currency that loses its purchasing power as the financial market fluctuates.

Even currencies have hard ones and soft ones?

A currency is not just money, it is power and strength, and its value depends on the demand from without and a country's ability from within to back up the face value.

6.   Conclusion

1997 - the coldest year for South Korea. More than four hundred Korean businessmen have committed suicide. On average, everyday there has been at least one person who has died because of this financial storm. However, we still optimistically believe that....

6.1 A New Model for East Asian Economic Growth

In the past, the nations of East Asia typically relied on export-led growth to earn foreign currency from the western nations and develop the domestic service sectors. This model had worked well in the past but is no longer viable for the developing nations of East Asia. East Asia now needs a new model for economic development.

In the previous chapter, I outlined the basis for this new development model. This model includes a focus on fostering core competencies, establishing a national financial management system on a par with international standards, and developing a financial defense system. At the same time, the model entails a reduction in investment in conventional industry and infrastructure, and calls for increased investment in a C&C society which includes a C&C industry, environment, and lifestyle.

The US which now boasts the highest per capita income in the world, is the world leader in the use of computer and networking equipment, and was the first country to enter into the information era. According to the most recent reports, the unemployment rate in the US has also fallen to an historical low of 4.6%. The economic success which the US has achieved makes me think back ten years ago to the book *World Challenge*. The book contained one key sentence which I will never forget: "The information age and knowledge-based economy of the future will create a labor shortage such that even our current global population of 5bn people will be insufficient to meet the demand for workers." I urge the leadership in East Asia to be carefully consider the implications of this prediction.

6.2   A Sense of Fatalism

The human cost of the recent turmoil in Asia must not be overlooked. There have been many sad stories as a result of the recent economic crisis. Businessmen in Korea have gone bankrupt, and pride and a strong sense of responsibility have pushed four hundred people in that country to take their lives - an average of over one suicide a day on a yearly basis. Even if the East Asian Financial Crisis was an historical inevitability, as a good neighbour we truly sympathise with those people in Korea who have been badly hurt by the crisis.

The worst thing that can happen in this or any financial crisis is a loss of confidence. In the medical profession, it is well known that many patients die not of illness but of losing confidence. Even healthy economies can collapse if participants lose confidence in the economy. While the greatest damage that has resulted from the East Asian Financial Crisis is reflected in Foreign Exchange losses and bankruptcies, the psychological damage the crisis caused is also significant. How a country and its people work together to build confidence will be the determining factor in smoothly getting through this crisis.

Let us pray for those who have suffered as a result of the economic crisis and may we all continue to create hope for the destiny and belief that:

There is an answer to every question.
There is a blessing in every obstacle.
There is a sunny sky that follows every storm.

Afterword

Is the East Asia financial crisis just another incident in the course of human history happening by chance, or is it inevitable destiny? What is the "the theory of Levorotation? What does this "Levorotary" theory have to do with the East Asian financial crisis?

The foreword to "the World of Fate"

By Sayling Wen

Approximately one year ago, at a breakfast meeting with Tsai Chih-chung, C.C. sketched his cartoons and at the same time explained the theory of levorotation that he had just come up with not long ago. Among all my friends and acquaintances, C.C. is the only one I know who can use words and pictures in combination to formulate ideas. He is able to approach problems from angles which most people would never consider.

At the time, I didn't really understand the thrust of what he was trying to communicate. I was struck, nonetheless, with the feeling that he was trying to formulate a prediction of the future.

After the East Asian Financial Crisis broke, we once again discussed the views that C.C. had tried to communicate over that breakfast meeting and we were amazed to find that the predictions he had made at that breakfast meeting fit very well with the events surrounding the financial crisis. Was the East Asian Financial Crisis a chance occurrence, or was it, in some strange way, pre-ordained? After all the analysis and hand-wringing is over, perhaps we will arrive at the conclusion that there was nothing that could have been done to avoid that crisis or other similar crises. Whether the crisis was preventable is perhaps a question that only history can answer.

The World of Fate

By Chih-Chung Tsai

Einstein said: "We believe that God is the underlying reason and force of the universe." The universe is circulating and moving according to a guideline of reason.... Perhaps we can look at this guideline in our search for humanity's path to our future destiny.

Prelude

Just like what Orwell tried to predict in his book *1984,* a British historian Arnold Tonybee predicted, East Asia will definitely rise again in the future. It already has a dominating importance in the world today, and to say that the 21st century is an Asian century is not an exaggeration.

At the same time, John Naisbitt, the world leader in trend prediction, has made an analysis of the East and West powers and how they will compare to each other in the future. He says that "at the dawn of the 21st century, there will be a central global force that will be the focus all over the world. This is the

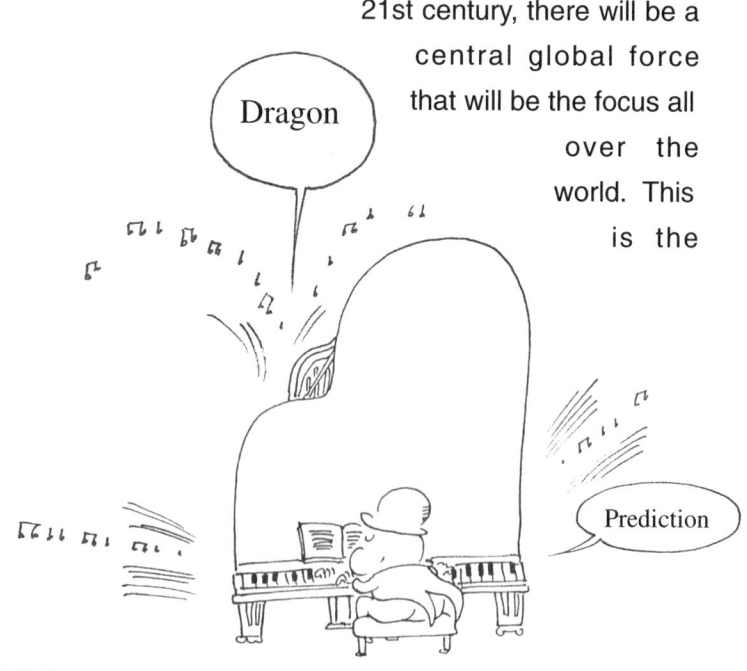

revival of the Giant Asian Dragon! For the Chinese people, the year 2000 is also the year of the Dragon, thus the beginning of the 'Dragon's Century' ."

Western scholars have predicted that Asia will be the most important region in the world in the 21st century. But even before this Asian century has arrived, Asia has suffered a tremendous fall. The financial destruction that resulted from the crisis as of the end of 1997 may have surpassed the financial destruction sustained throughout all of World War II. Is this new "Asian Century" going to fail even before it comes into existence, and will Asia say "sayonara" to the glorious title given to it by the Western scholars?

Mr. Greenspan, the Chairman of the American Federal Reserve Bank said, "In 1989 we saw the fall of Berlin Wall and the transformation of a planned economy into free market economy. Also as dramatic is the strong development of Asian capitalism that seems to be capable of competing in the free market economy. You can see from this the development of a certain framework. Even though I believe that there are flaws built in the system, as long as the Asian economies continue to grow at 10% annually, then these flaws will continue to be subdued." The flaw that Mr. Greenspan is referring to is the 'Asian Model.' It seems that the failure of the model is that it does not comply with the guidelines and principles of the western model, and the recent Asian financial storm seems to prove this point. Is the western method for a free market economy the only method for success? Is Asia destined to fail in its attempt to become the center stage for the world economy if it does not follow the western model? Is it part of the universal law which determines even the Earth's own motion that the world center is moving toward Asia?

The following is my analysis and vision. In the past, we Chinese were used to seeing the world through our own perspective, and what we called the world used to refer to the Western world. In ancient Greece there is a stone marker that indicates where the center of the world is. China, or "the Middle Kingdom," was named so because the Chinese believed that they were positioned at the center of the world. From a geological perspective of China, the East has a moist climate with forests, therefore east has a "wood" element. The west is arid and dry and therefore the element of the West is "metal." The heat of the south earns itself the element of "fire."

The north gets the element of "water" because of its cooler climate. The middle, where the Yellow Heights are located, without surprise, is considered to have the "soil" element.

China's concept of the five elements

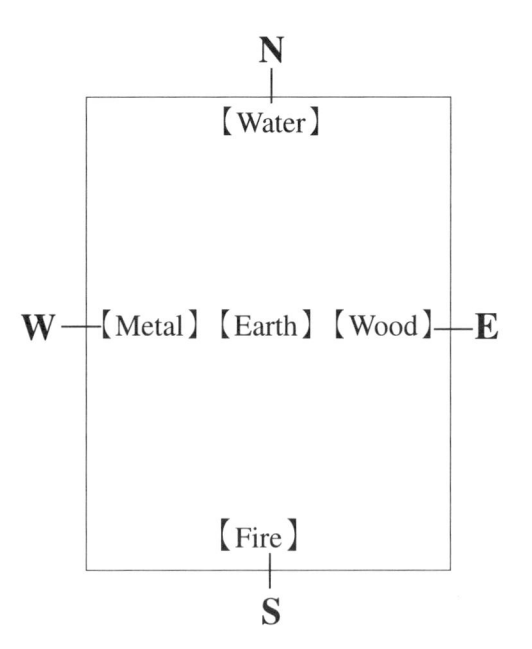

These 5 elements, which have long been a part of Chinese culture, came into existence naturally because we believe that we are located at the center of the world. This is a common perception in all humanity, because all people are looking from a single perspective. Both Eastern and Western countries are familiar with looking at history from their own position. However, one famous Chinese historian Ray Huang (黃仁宇) teaches us to really see the truth of history through a holistic perspective.

How did it happen? Why did it happen? What are the event's impacts? When Mr. Ren-Yu Huang refers to the macroscopic perspective of history, he is also referring to the three to five hundred years of influences that have directly and indirectly led up to and followed the actual event's occurrence.

Mr. Wen has discussed in great detail the causes of the Asian economic crisis and its impacts in the previous sections. Here, let us look at the whole issue of what has happened on the early with an even greater perspective of time and space. Perhaps we can then more clearly see the historical meaning of Asian financial crisis, and we can then try to understand the rhythm of the world of the 21st century.

Buddha says: "Whatever exists will change, and that whatever does not change does not exist. For changes to follow a set rhythm in motion is a set rule of the universe that cannot be changed."

The universe itself and everything in it all have a set element and a set rhythm for changes to take place. If we can see an event's past changes and detect its set rhythm, we can then see its future fluctuation from past events, and predict the future that it is hinting.

Those that follow the path will be pulled into the center of the past. Those that go against the path will move toward the direction of the future.

No matter where we are standing, even it is at the North or South Pole; the Earth is always rotating from west to east.

Ten thousand years ago, Polynesians from the South Pacific used their superior sailing technology and canoes to follow the Earth's rotation from West to East. They migrated by means of island hopping. As time went on, they eventually spread all over the areas now called Hawaii, Easter Island, Tahiti, and New Zealand. They successfully migrated to 2,500 uninhabited islands.

However, as time has gone on, Polynesians have not developed a more advanced culture. Instead, they have followed their ancestors and lived primitive lives. The "future" seems to have no meaning to these people.

Why is that?

Simply because they went the wrong way. The Earth is moving from west to east and following the Earth's rotation will only end up in the past. Only by moving toward the other direction or the world will one reach the future.

Example

When we go to work in a company, we will experience the rhythm and the guidelines of that company. If we follow the movement and adhere to all rules, we will eventually   to the core position within the company and become someone important.   If we do not follow the rhythm or rules and decide to go our own ways, we will either quit or be fired, thus having to start all over again.

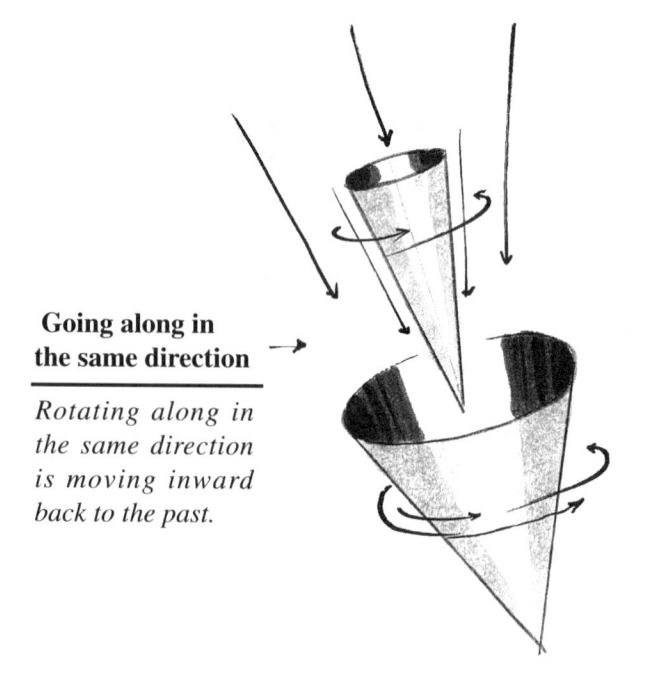

Going along in the same direction

Rotating along in the same direction is moving inward back to the past.

Why is that?

The current path only leads you to the destination and the core of the existing path. Only by going in the opposite direction and breaking the norm will you discover a new path, one that leads to the future.

Let's consider standing on the Northern Hemisphere. The earth is moving counterclockwise, and water always drains following a counterclockwise movement as it goes down into the earth. Vine plants, on the other hand, swirl up into the sky in a clockwise motion.

Because of the earth's rotation, from the Northern

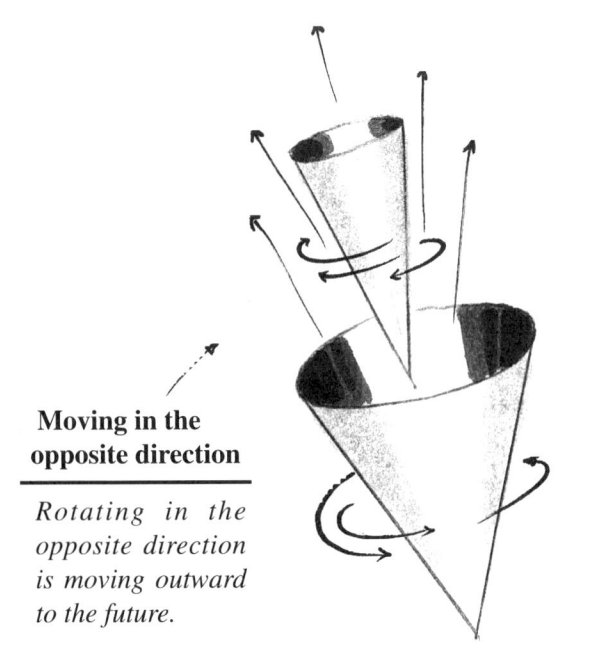

Moving in the opposite direction

Rotating in the opposite direction is moving outward to the future.

Hemisphere's perspective, a counterclockwise motion is from west to east. Therefore everything in the Northern Hemisphere follows a clockwise motion.

The "future" is to move in the opposite direction or the motion of the set path.

To go along in the same direction and the motion of the standing point will end up in the past.

Example

If we stand on a round plate rotating

N

Rotate clockwise

Rotate anti-clockwise

S

counterclockwise, because the outer area of the platform will rotate faster and move further than the inner areas, we will rotate clockwise, opposite to the platform, to balance ourselves.

The same principle applies to our atmosphere. Because of the uneven distribution of high and low-pressure weather systems, air currents flow from high pressure to low pressure systems. Because of the Earth's rotation — Coriolis will cause the air current to turn.

In the Northern Hemisphere from the perspective of the North Pole, the Earth is rotating

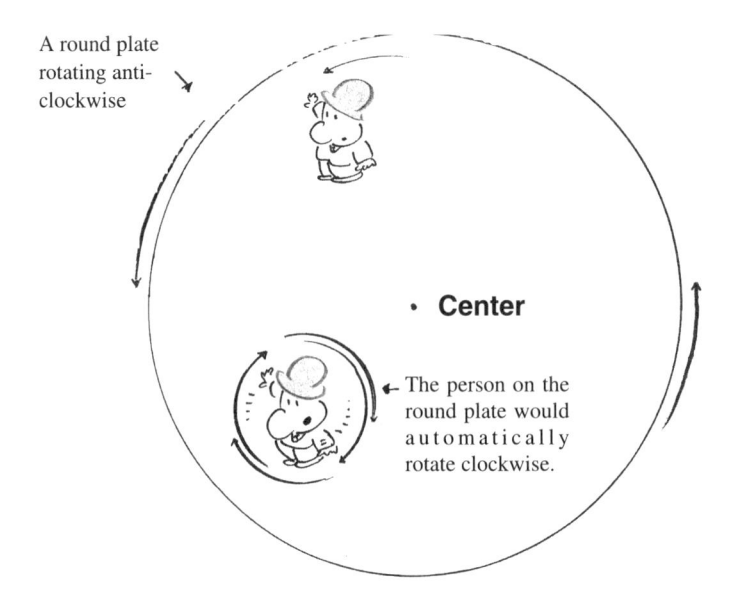

A round plate rotating anti-clockwise

• **Center**

← The person on the round plate would automatically rotate clockwise.

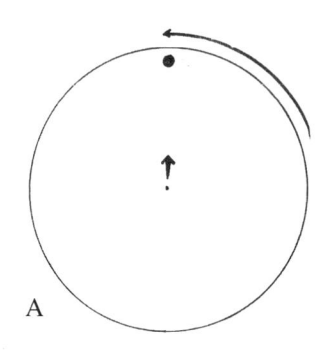

Picture A:

Shoot a bullet from Center C.

A moving cylinder will produce Coriolis effect.

What is Coriolis Force?
Coriolis Force, a force, resulting from the rotation of the Earth, that deflects other bodies or forces in motion, especially those above the Earth, by causing them to veer to the right in the Northern Hemisphere, or to the left in the Southern Hemisphere.

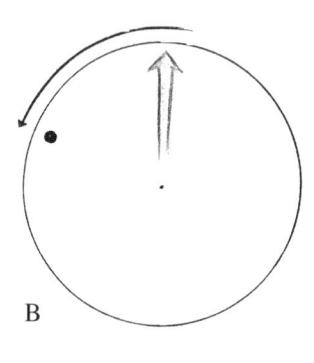

Picture B:

While the bullet is moving, Target T is also moving with the round plate. Since the bullet is still moving forward linearly, it will miss the target when it reaches the destination.

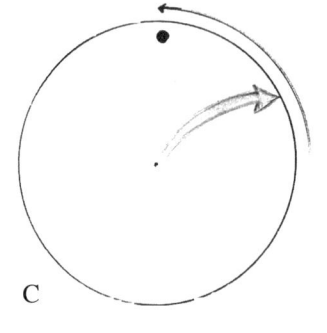

Picture C:

A person standing outside the plate can see clearly what's happening in picture A and B, whereas the people standing on point T and Point C see the course of the bullet as shown on Picture C, which is exactly what happens to the bullet moving on the round plate.

counterclockwise therefore air current flow out of high-pressure systems, turning in a clockwise rotation.

It is the opposite in the Southern Hemisphere. Looking from the South Pole, the Earth is rotating clockwise. When air currents moves away from high-pressure systems, they turn in counterclockwise rotation.

If we follow the movement of the surface plane we stand on, we will move to the center. On the other hand, if we move opposite to the surface plane, we will move away from the center and to the future.

From the Northern Hemisphere, the Earth has a counterclockwise rotation, therefore when someone on the Northern Hemisphere drains water; it has a counterclockwise swirl down into the Earth.

Any vine plant on the Northern Hemisphere grows toward the sun with a clockwise rotation, as if plants

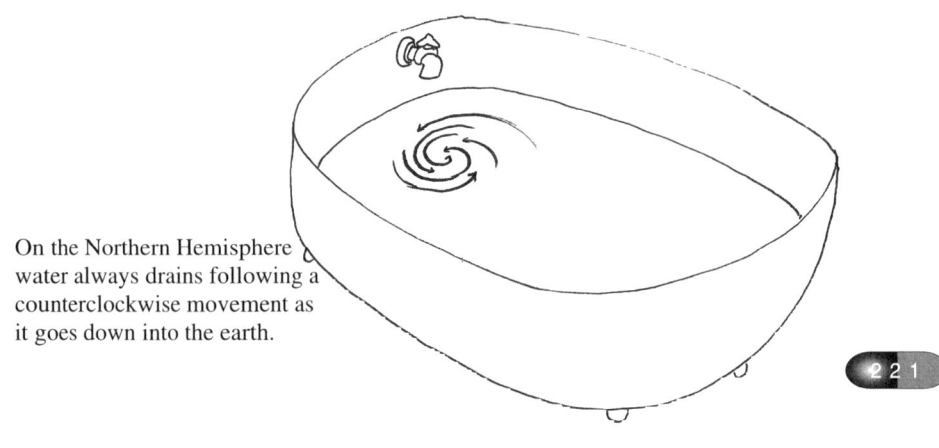

On the Northern Hemisphere water always drains following a counterclockwise movement as it goes down into the earth.

know physics without learning it.

In the Southern Hemisphere, the situation is the opposite. From the Southern Hemisphere the Earth has a clockwise rotation, therefore water drains down with a clockwise rotation, and vines grow up with a counterclockwise rotation.

From the above analysis we can come to the conclusion that to move in the same direction, as the standing point, is to go back to the past.

What is our standing point? The Earth. And where is the future of humanity? Most developed and

On the Northern Hemisphere vine plants swirl up into the sky in a clockwise motion.

developing countries are located in the Northern Hemisphere, therefore the Northern Hemisphere is relatively more wealthy than the Southern Hemisphere. Just like the uneven distribution of the atmosphere, uneven distribution of economic wealth will create a movement of people, and people move from poor land to rich land.

Right now the future development of the Southern Hemisphere is heading northward, but where is the future development of the Northern Hemisphere heading? From a Northern perspective, the Earth always rotates from west to east, thus the future of the Northern Hemisphere moves from east to west.

Moving Westward is the path of the Future

Following the established rhythm will only lead to

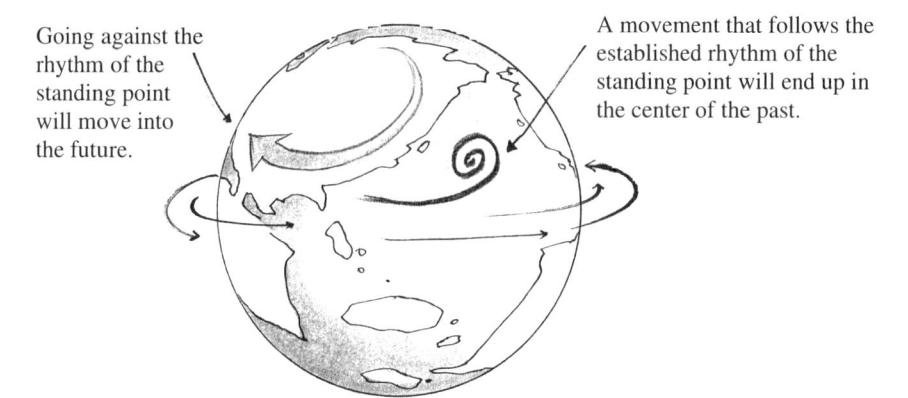

Going against the rhythm of the standing point will move into the future.

A movement that follows the established rhythm of the standing point will end up in the center of the past.

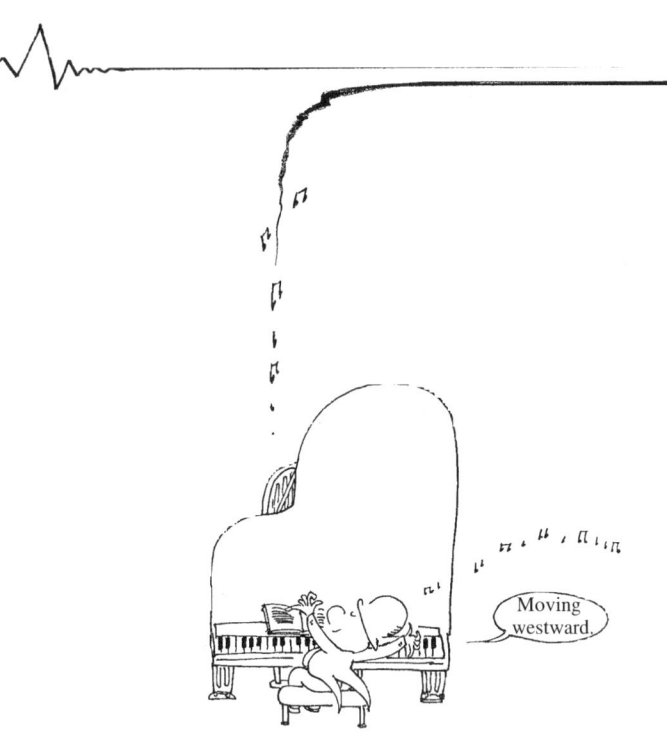

backward motions, only going against it can lead to the future. Because the Earth rotates from west to east, moving westward is the constant direction for moving into the future.

Five hundred years ago, after reading an old manuscript Columbus found that the Earth is round, and he concluded that sailing far into the ocean would not cause his ships to fall into a deep pit.

The silk and pottery from China and spices from India were Europeans' favorite items at the time. Even though China and India are to the East of Europe, Columbus believed that the Earth is round, and that he could reach India and China if he kept sailing west. Columbus convinced the Spanish queen, Queen Isabella, to fund his expedition. She did and he sailed off from the southern Spanish port of Palos. He successfully reached the West Indies on October 12, 1492 and discovered the New World.

Another great voyager Magellan sailed off with 5 Spanish ships going west on September 20, 1519. He passed the New World, sailing along Brazil, Argentina, through the now called Magellan Strait into the Pacific Ocean. Even though Magellan was killed in a battle with the natives in these foreign lands, his remaining crew of 18 returned to Spain on September 8, 1522 and accomplished the feat of circum navigating the world.

Although the Portuguese voyager Dias had reached the Cape of Good Hope of South Africa and had found a route to Japan in 1488, Columbus and

Magellan's desire was to sail west. Unknowingly, their voyages had a major impact on humanity's development. It seems that there is a subliminal desire in humans to travel west, and coincidentally the cultural development of many races is a historic path heading towards the west.

Over the last several thousand years, human development, both culturally and materialistically, has followed this path: the future relies on movement from east to west.

Six thousand years ago, the first human civilization was founded in what is modern day Syria, Iran, and Iraq. The Sumerian civilization and the later on Mesopotamian region and Babylonian kingdom, and the Egyptian Empire were all fertilized in the Middle East.

Two thousand six hundred years ago, world culture moved west from the Middle East, to Athens, Greece. Athens's philosophers and sages helped to shed the first light on human culture. Whether it is in physics, astronomy, mathematics, philosophy, or science, the influence of Athens still remains deeply embedded in modern society today.

Two thousand years ago, the center of the world

moved westward once again, this time to Rome. Be it politics, religion, or art, the Roman Empire had great influence over all of Europe and the Middle East for the subsequent 1,500 years.

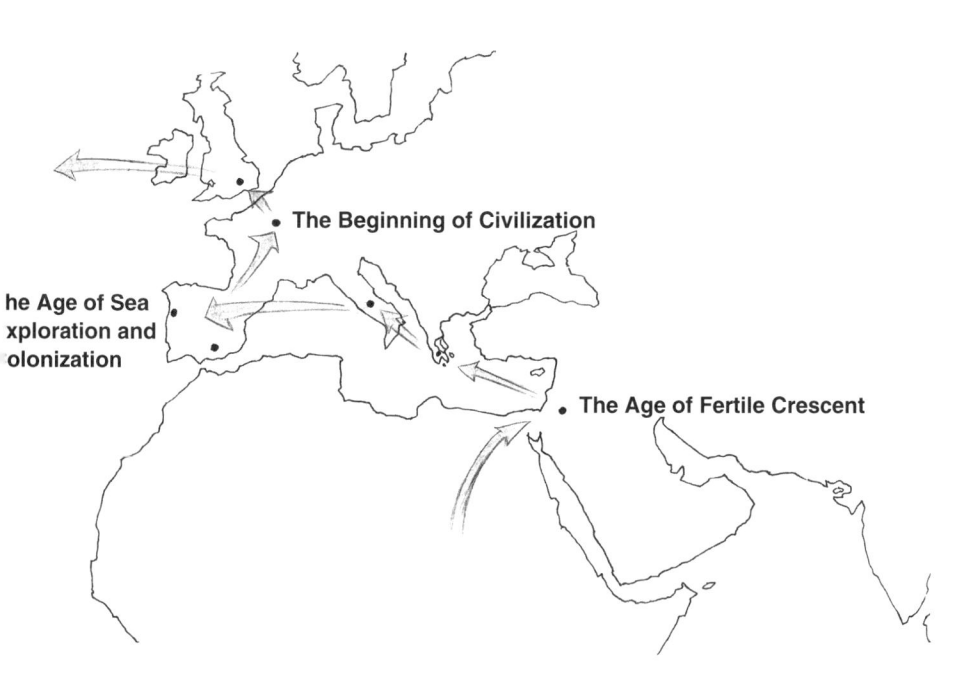

Five hundred years ago, the center of world moved to Spain and Portugal, and the age of exploration and colonization began. After the success of Columbus and Magellan, Spain and Portugal established vast colonies in Central and South America, the South Pacific, Southeast Asia, as well as Africa.

Two hundred years ago, the world's focus moved to France. Napoleon conquered Italy and Egypt and blockaded the European continent. His power covered almost all of Europe.

In 1815, the British defeated Napoleon at Waterloo, took the Cape of Good Hope, and extensively expanded colonies that included India, South Africa, Sri Lanka, Egypt, Malaysia and Myanmar, thus becoming the Kingdom where the sun never sets and the most powerful country in the 19th Century.

By 1945 World War II had ended, and because the U.S. was in a cold war with the Soviet Union, and Europe was in a stage of recovery, the U.S. became the most powerful country in the world. The center of the world at this point had crossed from Europe and moved to New York and Washington.

Thirty years ago, because of international trade, Japan's home appliance and automobile industries were exporting globally, and Japan was winning an economic war. It had managed to gain the most foreign reserves in the world as well as the world's highest surplus. At the same time, the U.S. was putting all its efforts into containing Communism. Internally the U.S. was having an economic recession.

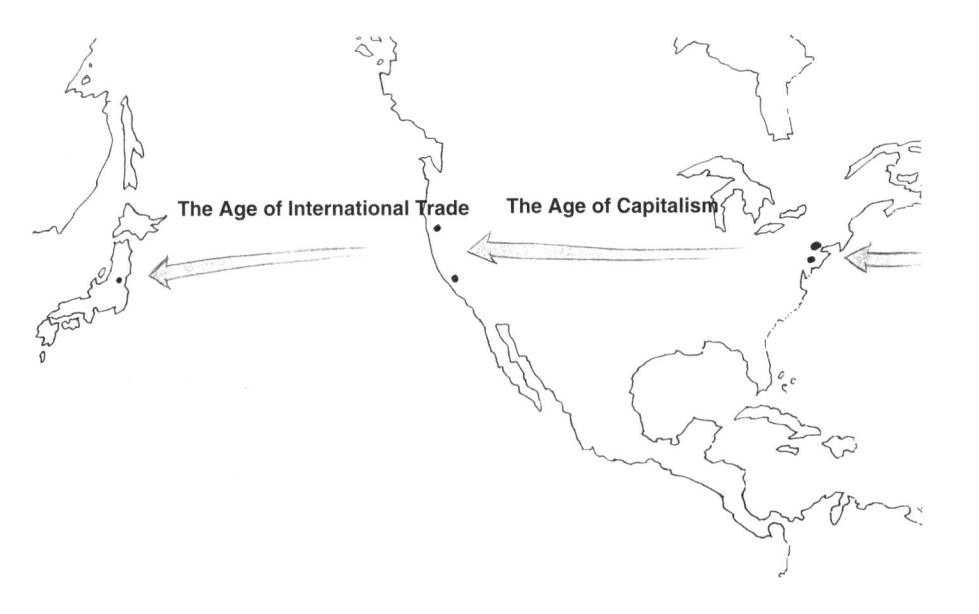

The Age of International Trade   The Age of Capitalism

At this point in time, the center stage had moved once again from New York, Washington to Tokyo.

Fifteen years ago, while Japan and the US were in economic competition in Asia; the computer and information age was on the rise. Because the US was willing to transfer its newest technology to independent suppliers in Asia, these products were able to compete directly with American and Japanese products. In addition, the collapse of the Japanese bubble economy set the stage for the rise of the four Asian Dragons: Taiwan, South Korea, Hong Kong, and Singapore.

Over the past ten years China has implemented many reforms, thus attracting a huge amount of foreign capital. By 1997, the value of Chinese foreign trade had reached USD$325 billion. Using their available natural resources and inexpensive human resources, the Chinese government is trying to move into the high-technology industry. In the future, China might establish stronger connections with Hong Kong, Taiwan, and Singapore, forming an alliance called "Greater China." This alliance could become an important manufacturing base for computer products sold all over the world.

Since 6000 years ago, the development of civilization, politics, and economy has been following a westward path. This path initially started in the Middle East and moved on to Athens, Rome, Spain, Portugal, Paris, London, New York, San Francisco, Los Angeles, Tokyo, Taipei, Seoul, Hong Kong, Singapore, and eventually to Beijing and Shanghai today.

The Age of Computer and Communications

Now at the dawn of the 21st century, the areas with the most promising growth are all Chinese. Accomplishments in Taiwan, Hong Kong, Singapore, and the China Mainland consider the following opinion as true: "the 21st century is Asia's century, and it will also be China's century..." And what about the Future?

Looking at the past, it can be seen how the mainstream of historic development in the Northern Hemisphere has always moved west. We can assume that the future will be no different. After the Chinese enjoy their attention as the focus of the world, history will be on the move again to the Himalayans. At that time, the age of BIO, a period where living quality and purity of the soul will be established. After the BIO age, the center of the world will move westward again, back to the Muslim world and the Guns and Roses age. One rotation will take 6000 years, and in the end, it will go right back to its original starting point, thus beginning once more.

Relationship between Point and Plane

What I have discussed has only focused on the movement of the focal point- the point at the tip of the arrow. The maintenance and disappearance of the "Plane" have not been covered.

After the focal point of the world has moved to Rome, the culture, chemistry, math, and religion of the Middle East still have influence over Rome. This is because the plane that the arrow sweeps over still covers the Middle East.

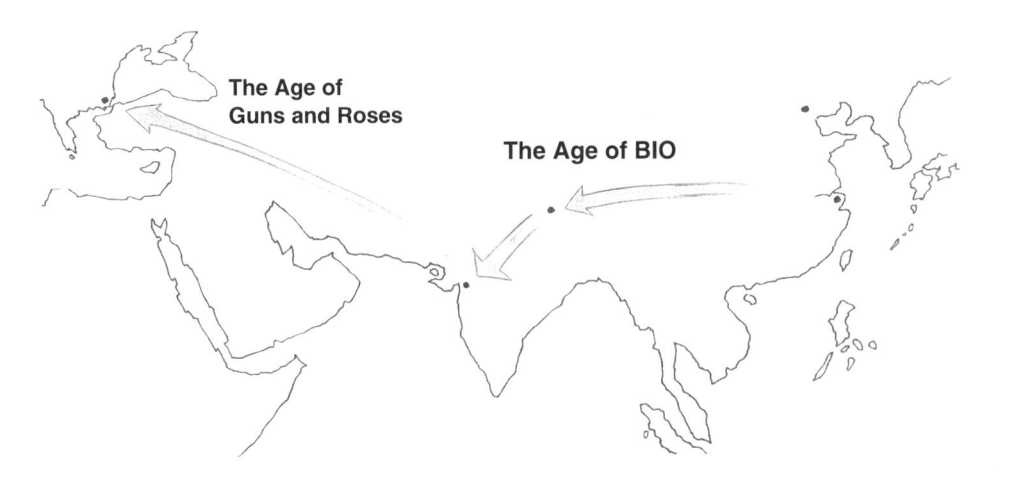

The Age of Guns and Roses

The Age of BIO

The arrow of the world center will constantly
move westward and soon pass today's center
which is likely to become yesterday's center.

Another example is how Americans have
managed to maintain their power and dominance
internationally and militarily even after the center has
moved to Asia. As long as it continues to play a crucial
part in keeping world order and dominating global
trade, it will not lose its influence. Thus, it will maintain
a healthy relationship with the focal point and form a
plane of co-prosperity.

It is only the center, or the new focus of the world
that will keep moving west. If the previous center
continues developing and maintaining its strength and
influence, it can always form a co-prosperity plane by

maintaining a healthy interaction with the focal point at various times.

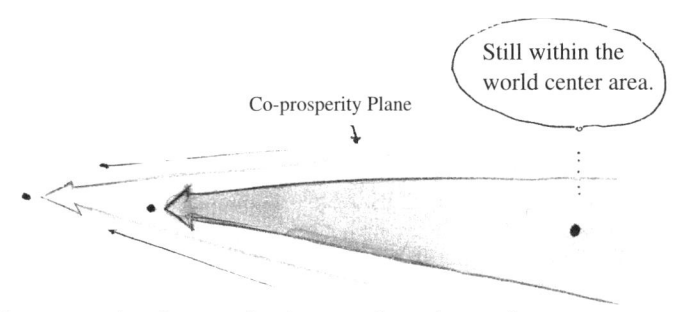

If the arrow tip of yesterday keeps advancing and growing, it will be able to interact positively with the point the arrow reaches and form a plane of co-prosperity.

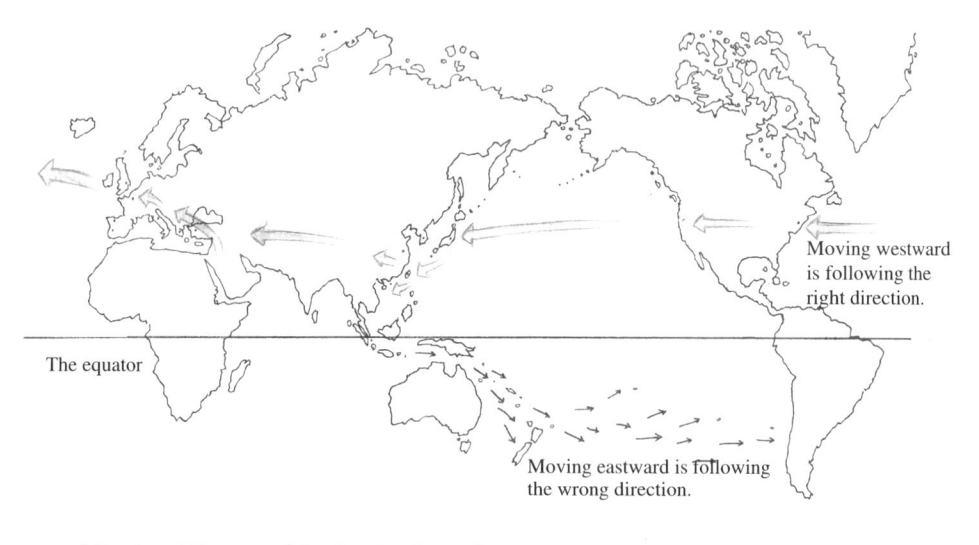

Moving westward is following the right direction.

The equator

Moving eastward is following the wrong direction.

Moving Westward Is the Path to the Future

Whether or not you believe this, the development of humanity, in cultural and in technological development, is a historic path that is constantly going westward.

Going west is often an easier path that bestows great results. On the contrary, going east is often met with challenges and difficulties that may cause one's efforts to be fruitless. There are numerous cases in history that support this belief.

For example, Genghis Khan's expedition westward in the 13th century was able to conquer almost the whole Eurasia continent, and it didn't seem very difficult. However, after his heirs were able to maintain control of China, they attacked Japan twice, with both attempts to conquer the Japanese ending in failure.

As for Japanese history, it has always been the northern and eastern warlords who have defeated and dominated the southern and western warlords. Japan was also easily able to take over China and Southeast Asia because it was going westward. However, when Japan had a war on its own eastern front, it lost to the U.S.

Even historical records that exist have this tendency. Bartolomeu Dias was the first man to reach the southern tip of Africa and South America, but because Magellan was going west, he is remembered the most. Later people even named a constellation after him.

The Borderless Future

The future will be different from the past. Due to the establishment of global information networks, such as the Internet and telecommunications systems and the push for a global capital revolution, a borderless single global market may appear in the future.

In the 19th century, Europe called China a "Sleeping Lion." Napoleon is quoted as saying: "Do not wake the lion in the East."

Today, the lion has awoken! And it is a coincidence that at the turn of the century the focus has been moved to Asia. Taiwan, Hong Kong, Singapore, China, and ethnic Chinese in many Southeast Asian countries are forming a Greater China network, and are ready to walk into the Century of the Dragon as they approach the year 2000. Yet at this crucial moment, the East Asian financial storm is happening. Will this cause Asian or Chinese dominance to disappear?

Following the 6000-year analysis that I have derived, the westward movement will not stop and go back to Europe or America. It will be like Magellan's voyage, despite his death in the Philippines, his voyage was still successful in the end.

The East Asian economic crisis has created great negative impacts. All countries except for China have either fallen or have been affected. The Currencies of many countries have depreciated 40% to 50% and even Japan and Asia's Dragons have been affected. However, everything has a negative and positive side. We should not only look carefully at the negative impacts of the economic crisis, but we should also look at the positive side too.

In this global economy, the international investors that are playing short-term games can be considered

Bright Side

Dark Side

predators. In nature, predators kill weaker animals for food and affect the whole environment. Investors partake in market activities to gain maximum profits, leaving countries with injuries and casualties. From a biological standpoint, predators are necessary in nature to maintain a population balance for all species. Predators also play another important role. They help maintain the health and ability of the prey.

Predators usually go after the weak, the old, and the sick. This helps decrease the number of weaker prey, and the ones that are left breed stronger and more able offspring. This is very beneficial to all species from an evolutionary standpoint.

The same analogy can be applied to the global business world. Short-term investors are always looking for markets where interest rates and asset prices are not at normal rate. They come in forcefully and then exit after they have gained great profit, leaving institutions that were already unhealthy even more vulnerable. Short-term investors also force some countries to change policies that were already unreasonable leading to corruption and lack of efficiency.

Because of the existence of the financial predator,

Decrease in preys
gives the grassland
a chance to come
alive and expand.

Increase in grass**lands**
causes increase in **grass-**
eating preys.

No chance to hunt
other animals for
food,

As grass-eating preys
decrease little by little,
the predators decrease
with their food source.

Increase in grass-**eating**
preys causes **increases**
in predators.

But the existence of predator
causes a decrease in grass-
eating preys.

Not enough
grassland for us,

**The Triangular
Relationship among Preys,
Predators and Grassland
– Ecological Equilibrium**

Too many grass-eating prey
cause grassland to decrease.

businesses worldwide need to learn how to react quickly to market changes, thus lending to a better infrastructure and framework in order to move into the global market of the 21st century. This worldwide business and institutional optimization exemplifies the economic crisis's benefits. .

At the dawn of the 21st century, the world is moving towards a single global market. Under capitalist revolution pressure, a perfectly competitive market is beginning to surface. No one will be able to place himself or herself outside this market system, and there won't be anyone who can survive independently in a way that goes against this kind of market.

The East Asian financial storm should be considered a warning sign telling people to be prepared to enter the global market. It can also be considered a prelude to the coming millenium.

Whether our future is heading towards prosperity or destruction will depend on whether or not we can sense the hidden meanings inside this warning sign. If we can understand the meaning and use it to keep ourselves alert and constantly improving, while internally maintaining a healthy system and externally paying more attention to global market changes and what they are telling us, then we can succeed and prosper in this borderless future.

Ordinary people are controlled by fate Wise people create fate

Two thousand five hundred years ago, an ancient Indian saint told his disciple A-Nan: " Rely on yourself, rely on the truth of the Universe; be your own light; you yourself determine what your path is. Everyone should be their own deliverance; no one in the world other than himself can bring himself salvation; therefore everyone should work hard to go forward without losing their own diligence."

Throughout history's evolution, humanity has been the most important element and variable. It is the intentions and the actions of man that will dictate any creation or destruction. Ordinary man is controlled by fate, whereas it is the wise man that creates his own fate. Man dictates the speed and time of fate's circulation. The fact that the arrow of fate, or the point of focus, has reached us does not determine how long the focal point will stay with us. It also does not tell us how much prosperity will
be created for us. Everything depends upon what we do.

We are fortunate to be living in this great era where we are able to create our own history with our fate. If we keep in our heart and mind the words that Buddha has passed down to us, internally purify ourselves and externally observe the truth of the Universe, then we can work together hand-in-hand and embrace the " New Asian Millennium."

Appendix 1

My friend Steven Wu graduated from National Taiwan University, and received his MBA from the National Cheng Chi University. He is currently studying for his doctorate in finance at Boston University and serves as Chief Secretary of the Small and Medium Enterprise Administration of Ministry of Economic Affairs. He works nearly every day from 7:00AM until 11:00PM at night and is outstanding in almost every way, but especially in his professionalism and dedication to his work. He was especially prized by late Central Bank Governor Mr. Sheu Yuan-dong. Much of the information which follows was prepared by Steven, and I would like to take this opportunity to offer special thanks to him for all his considerable efforts.

(by Sayling Wen)

Governor Sheu Yuan-dong: In Memoriam

By Steven Wu

"In the misty days of March, azaleas bloom on the mountainsides, azaleas bloom on the riversides....." Having survived the East Asian Financial Crisis with its competitive strength still intact, Taiwan's corporate sector stands out through the cold and snow of the region's turbulence just like a pine tree in a winter landscape. Taiwan corporations now greet the region's spring and summer with a renewed exuberance and vigor. During this period of rebirth, it is especially painful to recognize that one of the men who ensured Taiwan's safe passage through the East Asian Financial Crisis, the late Central Bank Governor Mr. Sheu Yuan-dong, along with his wife and four colleagues perished in the line of duty in a plane crash upon their return from the annual Asian Central Bank Governor's conference. While Mr. Sheu's tragic passing remains painful, his works live on, and through this book we memorialize him.

I recall clearly in 1994, when Mr. Sheu was Chairman of the Bank of Taiwan, which Mr. Sheu felt strongly that Taiwanese investors in Southeast Asia were in need of additional financial assistance. At that time, Mr. Sheu invited Sayling Wen and three or four others with experience in offshore investment to attend a seminar at the bank. Mr. Sheu requested that all the officers in the bank's headquarters and all the managers in the bank's branches attend the meeting. The meeting itself last for three and a half hours, and the Governor attended the entire session, taking notes assiduously throughout. During a break midway through the seminar, Mr. Sheu remarked that during the period of Japanese occupation, the Bank of Taiwan had established a network of branches throughout Southeast Asia, but after Taiwan's return to China, the network of overseas branches was shut down. Mr. Sheu felt that it was imperative that the bank reopen its network of overseas branches and accelerate the pace of internationalization. Upon hearing Mr. Sheu's thoughts, I was deeply struck by his far-sightedness. All of the overseas branches which the Bank of Taiwan operates at present, were in fact either opened or planned during Mr. Sheu's tenure as Chairman. His contribution to the Bank of Taiwan and the nation indeed must not be underestimated.

As Governor of the Central Bank, the needs of

industry were always at the forefront of his concerns. On several occasions, I called to Mr. Sheu's attention Sayling Wen's views on the development of the high-tech industry. I also provided Mr. Sheu all five of Sayling Wen's works: *Industry Transplantation, Success with Money & Joy, Prospect, Enterprise Acceleration, and Taiwan Experience.* After reading these works, the Governor arranged to meet with Sayling and myself. That was on August 1, 1997 during the time of the rapid depreciation of the Thai Baht and the beginning of the East Asian Financial Crisis. The Taiwanese financial markets were also uneasy at the time, and prior to our meeting that day Governor Sheu had carefully gathered the opinions of leaders in government and industry in formulating Taiwan's financial strategy.

The Governor was in buoyant sprits as we met, and had read all five of Sayling Wen's books. As such, he had a strong appreciation for Sayling's experience and the ingredients of his success. We discussed at length the issues surrounding the East Asian Financial Crisis. During our discussion I was particularly struck with the Governor's dedication to his work, his deep patriotic feelings, and his sense of mission. I was also overwhelmed to discover that I had encountered a man not only of great wisdom, knowledge and technical proficiency in financial affairs, but also a man filled with warmth and powerful feelings of aesthetic appreciation. He was a true gentleman and a great pillar of the nation.

On January 6, 1998, Sayling Wen and I attended a seminar hosted by the Chung-Hua Institution for Economic Research. The seminar was devoted to the East Asian Financial Crisis. Governor Sheu also attended the seminar as a speaker. At the seminar, the Governor detailed the Central Bank's policy throughout the crisis, and the decision-making process behind the Central Bank policy. All in attendance were highly edified by his detailed recount of those historic events. During a break in the seminar, many approached the Governor to discuss his views in greater detail, and I can picture him now just as he was, smiling warmly as was his nature.

When Sayling Wen finished this book on January 23, 1998, he provided me with a draft to give to Governor Sheu. The Governor read the manuscript and was very encouraging, asking many probing questions and displaying strong interest in Sayling's line of reasoning. He also mentioned that he would be happy to write the foreword for the book. Thinking back, with Mr. Sheu now departed from us forever, his foreword is now just a distant memory but one that will remain with us in our hearts and imagination.

On February 12, on the afternoon of the day the Governor left for Indonesia to attend the annual Asian Central Bank Governor's Meeting, he instructed the late Chief of the Bureau of Monetary Affairs, Mr. Chen Huang, to contact Sayling Wen. The two were to discuss how best the Taiwan government could assist Taiwanese investors in Southeast Asia caught in the midst of the financial crisis. Unfortunately, Sayling was overseas, and by the time he had contacted the Central Bank, Mr. Chen had already left for Indonesia.

On February 16th, just as Governor Sheu was preparing to leave Indonesia to return to Taiwan, he contacted his secretary in Taiwan to ask if there were any pressing matters at hand. This was to be his last phone call on public matters. His secretary notified him that a Taiwanese businessman in Indonesia had submitted a request for financial assistance as the financial crisis had rendered him unable to raise adequate amounts of working capital. Governor Sheu then requested that his secretary quickly fax the request to him in Indonesia. After understanding the request, he asked Mr. Chen to contact the Taiwanese businessman who had sent the request. This was Governor Sheu, always ready to be of help to those in need. When I later learned of these, the Governor's last acts, I was overwhelmed with fond remembrances of this great man and great friend. Indeed, words are insufficient to express my admiration for him.

Sayling Wen and I were fortunate to have known Governor Sheu and to have learned much from him. We are also grateful for the generous support which the Governor lent us on many occasions, and thus we dedicate this book to him.

Governor Sheu, may your spirit never die, and may you always live on in our memories.

Appendix 2

Exhibit 1. Economic Growth Rate for Main Areas of the World (%)

	1996	1997	1998 (predicted)
Global	2.5	3.1	2.5
North America	2.7	3.8	2.7
West Europe	1.7	2.5	2.7
Asia Pacific	4.6	2.7	1.2
Latin America	3.5	5.0	3.2

Source: Chung-Hua Institution for Economic Research

Exhibit 2. Economic Growth Rate for Top Seven Industrial Countries (%)

	1997	1998 (predicted)
US	3.8	2.7
Japan	1.0	0.1
Canada	3.7	3.3
England	3.4	2.3
France	2.4	2.8
Italy	1.4	2.3
Germany	2.3	2.7

Source: Same as Exhibit 1

Exhibit 3. GDP Growth Rate for Asian Countries (%)

	1994	1995	1996	1997	1998 (predicted)
Thailand	8.9	8.8	6.0	-0.5	-3.5
Malaysia	9.2	9.5	8.2	6.8	2.0
Indonesia	7.5	8.2	8.0	5.0	-2.1
Philippines	4.4	4.8	5.5	4.7	3.0
South Korea	8.6	8.9	7.1	4.9	-2.0
ROC	6.5	6.0	5.7	6.3	5.1
Hong Kong	5.4	4.5	4.9	5.4	3.4
Singapore	10.5	8.8	7.0	7.6	2.6
China	12.6	9.0	9.7	8.8	8.4

Source: WEFA, World Economic Outlook, Jan. 1998

Remark: Each country's GDP is based on the exchange rate against the USD, 1990

Exhibit 4. GDP Before and After the Financial Crisis (%)

	1996		1998 *	
	GDP (billion USD)	Exchange rate for the year	GDP(billion USD)	Exchange rate on Feb. 4th
Thailand	186	25.34	97	48.75
Malaysia	92	2.52	71	3.922
Indonesia	226	2,342	51	9,000
Philippines	84	26.22	68	40.22
South Korea	485	804.5	272	1,609
ROC	272	27.26	269	32.9
Hong Kong	154	7.73	188	7.7355
Singapore	94	1.41	92	1.6675
China	839	8.31	1,063	8.31

Source: a. Economist, Feb. 7th-13th, 1998
  b. Peregrine
  c. WEFA, World Economic Outlook, Jan. 1998
Remark: Each country's GDP of 1998 is based on the exchange rate against the USD, Feb. 4th, 1998.

Exhibit 5. Yearly Incremental Rate of
Consumer Price Index for Asian Countries   (%)

	1997	1998	Jan. 1998
ROC	0.9	3.1	1.8
Thailand	5.6	11.0	8.6
Malaysia	2.6	6.2	3.4
Indonesia	6.6	23.7	18.1
Philippines	8.4	10.4	6.4
South Korea	4.4	9.8	8.3
Hong Kong	5.8	4.6	4.6
Singapore	2.0	2.8	1.2
China	2.8	3.5	0.3

Source: same as Exhibit 1

Exhibit 6.1. Import, Export and Current Account
for Asian Countries

(Billion USD, %)

		Thailand		Malaysia		Indonesia		Philippine		South Korea	
		Amount	Growth Rate	Amount	Growth Rate	Amount	Growth Rate	Amount	Growth Rate	Amount	Growth Rate
Export	1995	55.4	24.7	72.1	26.6	45.5	13.1	17.4	29.4	123.2	31.5
	1996	54.4	-1.9	77.0	6.8	49.8	9.5	20.5	17.8	128.3	4.1
	1997	55.5	2.0	79.2	2.9	54.4	9.3	25.5	24.4	137.8	7.4
	1998	59.3	6.8	87.2	10.2	60.1	10.5	30.6	20.0	151.9	10.2
Import	1995	63.4	31.6	72.2	30.4	39.8	23.0	26.4	23.7	127.9	32.1
	1996	68.9	0.8	73.7	2.2	43.0	8.2	32.8	24.4	143.6	12.2
	1997	55.8	-12.6	76.3	3.6	42.2	-2.0	36.0	11.6	140.9	-1.9
	1998	53.6	-4.0	82.4	7.9	40.1	-5.0	39.0	6.6	135.5	-3.8
Trade Balance	1995	-8.0		-0.1		5.7		-8.9		-4.7	
	1996	-0.5		3.3		6.8		-12.3		-15.3	
	1997	-0.3		2.8		12.8		-11.2		3.1	
	1998	5.6		4.9		20.1		-8.4		16.4	
Current Account	1995	-13.6		-7.4		-7.0		-2.0		-8.3	
	1996	-14.7		-3.6		-7.0		-4.8		-23.1	
	1997	-3.4		-4.8		-2.2		4.0		-8.8	
	1998	1.8		-2.8		4.0		-0.3		8.1	

(The 1998 data is predicted data)
Source: WEFA, World Economic Outlook, Jan. 1998

Exhibit 6.2. Import, Export and Current Account for Asian Countries (Billion USD, %)

		ROC		Hong Kong		Singapore		China	
		Amount	Growth Rate	Amount	Growth Rate	Amount	Growth Rate	Amount	Growth Rate
Export	1995	111.2	19.9	173.8	14.8	118.5	21.0	128.1	24.9
	1996	115.5	3.8	180.7	4.0	126.0	6.4	147.5	15.2
	1997	121.6	5.3	187.6	3.8	126.8	0.6	180.5	22.4
	1998	134.3	10.5	195.1	4.0	138.2	9.0	191.2	5.9
Import	1995	98.0	21.2	192.8	19.1	117.4	21.6	110.1	15.5
	1996	97.9	-0.1	198.5	8.0	123.7	5.4	127.9	16.2
	1997	108.5	10.8	208.7	5.1	125.7	1.0	134.8	5.3
	1998	120.7	11.3	214.9	3.0	137.1	9.0	149.9	11.2
Trade Balance	1995	13.2		19.0		5.7		18.1	
	1996	17.6		-17.8		6.8		19.6	
	1997	13.1		-21.1		12.8		45.8	
	1998	13.6		-19.8		20.1		41.3	
Current Account	1995	5.5		-4.3		-7.0		1.6	
	1996	11.0		-1.1		-7.0		10.7	
	1997	3.7		-4.3		-2.2		29.5	
	1998	4.0		-2.1		4.0		20.4	

(1998 data is predicted data)
Source: WEFA, World Economic Outlook, Jan. 1998

Exhibit 7. Surplus of Current Account
for Asian Countries   (Billion USD)

	1997	1998 (predicted)
ROC	6.8	5.3
Thailand	-4.1	3.8
Malaysia	-4.8	-2.6
Indonesia	-6.6	-0.4
Philippines	-3.4	-2.2
South Korea	-9.9	2.7
Hong Kong	-4.6	-4.3
Singapore	12.4	11.7
China	22.5	17.2

Source: Same as Exhibit 1

**Exhibit 8. FDI Proportion of Current Account
in Southeast Asian Countries** (%)

	1993	1994	1995	1996
ROC	13.73	22.26	32.50	17.71
Thailand	-67.62	-73.09	-120.88	-75.69
Malaysia	-35.00	-40.00	-17.53	-40.82
Indonesia	-387.62	-847.14	-570.14	-369.43
Philippines	-41.33	-56.33	-76.00	-26.36
Singapore	111.67	74.07	54.37	66.48
China	-237.24	475.22	2,240.63	558.06

Source: Taiwan Institute of Economic Research

Exhibit 9. Foreign Reserves for Asian Countries (Billion USD)

	Jan, 1998	Jan, 1997
ROC	83.1	87.7
Thailand	26.2	37.7
Malaysia	21.7	27
Indonesia	18.9	15.7
Philippines	8.8	9.7
South Korea	21.1	34
Hong Kong	96.5	63.8
Singapore	74.5	75
China	141.3	104.3

Source: Same as Exhibit 1

Exhibit 10. Foreign Debt and Repayment Proportion
of Exports for Asian Countries (Billion USD %)

		Thailand		Malaysia		Indonesia		Philippines		South Korea	
		Amount	Growth Rate	Amount	Growth Rate	Amount	Growth Rate	Amount	Growth Rate	Amount	Growth Rate
Foreign Debt Balance	1995	56.8	18.1	34.4	16.6	107.8	11.7	39.4	-1.5	78.4	37.8
	1996	63.4	11.6	39.2	14.0	113.1	4.9	42.0	6.6	104.7	33.5
	1997	57.4	-9.5	38.1	-2.8	123.1	8.8	45.7	8.8	120.8	15.4
	1998	62.1	8.2	36.6	-3.9	127.8	3.8	49.9	9.2	119.4	-1.2
Repayment Proportion of Exports	1995	30.7		14.8		63.0		39.4		5.4	
	1996	38.0		15.1		67.6		28.8		5.8	
	1997	40.4		17.9		65.6		28.7		5.1	
	1998	27.1		16.8		73.9		28.0		4.9	

		ROC		Hong Kong		Singapore		China	
		Amount	Growth Rate	Amount	Growth Rate	Amount	Growth Rate	Amount	Growth Rate
Foreign Debt Balance	1995	—	—	—	—	—	—	118.1	17.5
	1996	—	—	—	—	—	—	128.5	8.8
	1997	—	—	—	—	—	—	138.2	7.5
	1998	—	—	—	—	—	—	152.5	10.3
Repayment Proportion of Exports	1995	—		—		—		21.4	
	1996	—		—		—		22.9	
	1997	—		—		—		19.8	
	1998	—		—		—		20.0	

(1998 data is predicted data)
Source: WEFA, World Economic Outlook, Jan. 1998

Exhibit 11. Economic Indicators before the Financial Crisis for Southeast Asian Countries, Compared with those of Mexico in 1994.

	1996					1994
	Thailand	Malaysia	Indonesia	Philippines	Singapore	Mexico
Current Account Proportion of GDP, %	-11.2	-8.7	-4	-8.4	23.8	-9.9
Foreign Debt Proportion of GDP, %	60.7	53	53	84.3	—	43.5
Short Term Debt Proportion of Foreign Reserves	—	87.2	127.9	75.7	—	20
Months of Foreign Exchange that can be provided for import needs, (months)	6.8	7.3	5.0	6.7	7.4	0.9
(FDI + Current Account) Proportion of GDP, %	-9.0*	-2.0*	-1.6*	-1.0*	39.0*	-6.2

Source: Taiwan Institute of Economic Research
Remark: * is the 1995 data

Exhibit 12. Exchange Rate against USD for Asian Countries

	End of 1996	End of 1997	2nd March, 1998
ROC	27.50	32.67	32.05
Thailand	25.61	48.15	43.55
Malaysia	2.53	3.89	3.64
Indonesia	2,348.00	4,375.00	8,750.00
Philippines	26.29	39.90	39.75
South Korea	844.20	1,695.00	1,555.00
Hong Kong	7.74	7.75	7.74
Singapore	1.40	1.69	1.62
China	8.30	8.28	8.28

Source: Chung-Hua Institution for Economic Research

Exhibit 13. Performance of Stock Market Before and After Financial Storm for Asian Countries

	Stock Index		Change of Stock Index (%)
	8th Jan. 1997	10th Dec. 1997	
Thailand	831.90	390.70	-53.4
Malaysia	1,239.50	636.40	-48.66
Indonesia	662.20	415.90	-37.19
Philippines	3,207.00	1,972.80	-38.48
South Korea	621.40	399.90	-35.65
ROC	7,019.40	8,503.60	21.14
Hong Kong	13,454.90	11,022.40	-18.08
Singapore	2,243.30	1,703.50	-24.06
China	935.70	1,217.50	30.12

Source: Same as Exhibit 1

Exhibit 14. Average Wage per Month per capita of Manufacturing Industries for Asian Countries (USD)

	1992	1993	1994	1995	1996
ROC	1,072.02	1,092.42	1,161.26	1,225.11	1,229.61
Malaysia	311.37	329.96	—	—	—
Philippines	211.13	205.90	—	—	—
South Korea	1,022.93	1,103.07	1,272.64	1,457.21	—
Singapore	1,034.48	1,122.10	1,304.12	1,519.23	1,645.39
China	935.70	48.44	41.41	51.59	—

Source: Taiwan Institute of Economic Research

A *tomorrow* Book

Locus Publishing Company

Taipei County, Taiwan

2-3, Alley 20, Lane 142, Sec. 6, Roosevelt Road, Taipei, Taiwan

ISBN 957-8468-46-6 Chinese Language Edition

ISBN 957-8468-81-4 English Language Edition

Copyright ©1998 by Sayling Wen &Tsai Chi-Chung

April 1999, First Edition

Printed in Taiwan

tomorrow10
You Too Can Understand -
The East Asian Financial Crisis

作者：溫世仁　繪圖：蔡志忠

英譯：Jonathan Ross

編輯：明日工作室

出版者：大塊文化出版股份有限公司

法律顧問：全理律師事務所董安丹律師

台北市117羅斯福路六段142巷20弄2-3號

電話：(02)29357190　傳真：(02)29356037

e-mail:locus@locus.com.tw

信箱：新店郵政16之28號信箱

讀者服務專線：080-006689

郵撥帳號：**18955675** 帳戶名：大塊文化出版股份有限公司

行政院新聞局局版北市業字第706號

總經銷：北城圖書有限公司　　地址：台北縣三重市大智路139號

電話：(02)9818089(代表號) 傳真：(02)9883028 9813049

製版印刷：源耕印刷事業有限公司

初版一刷：1999年4月　　定價：新台幣180元

明日工作室 策劃
溫世仁・蔡志忠
監製

你能懂

2小時掌握一個知性主題

生命複製

You Got It!

吳宗正/著

何文榮/著

　　近一年來，有關「生命」方面的訊息，持續不斷地匯入我們的思維與生活中，先是發生在英國的狂牛症，其次是發生在國內的口蹄疫，再來是複製羊「桃莉」的誕生，這種「無性生殖」的成功，讓人立刻聯想到複製人的可行性，甚至已不是可能不可能的問題，而是已經面臨做不做的抉擇了。而其引發的後續有關的道德、倫理、與法律規範問題，更是如波濤洶湧般，激起大家的警覺。另外，冷凍人的問題，代理孕母的問題，加上重大刑案、華航空難所牽涉的DNA鑑定問題，這一連串事件接踵發生，媒體的推波助瀾，彷彿接下來就是生物科技的世紀，也就是說「基因的世紀」就在我們跟前　然而我們捫心自問，我們對基因、對生命，究竟瞭解多少？本書將以輕鬆愉快，簡單易懂的方式，逐步引導讀者認識「生命」，尤其是百分之九十五以上未受過生命科學洗禮的國人，更需補充這方面的知識。如此才能在即將來臨，且肯定會涉入我們未來生活，甚或如影隨形地影響我們一生的「基因世紀」，具備與生命科學家互通的共同語言，進一步參與對話及討論，並擁有足夠的知識來做正確的價值判斷。

你能懂

2小時掌握一個知性主題

多媒體

You Got It!

鄒景平
侯延卿 合著

二十一世紀是多媒體與網路結合的新世紀，它為我們生活、工作、學習及育樂交誼型態帶來莫大的衝擊，也將對商務交易、企業運作、都市生活型態產生革命性的影響。多媒體普及之後，人類的思考模式、社會文化、居住型態及環境生態也都會隨之改變。

就像女星珊卓・布拉克（Sandra Bullock）主演的電影《網路上身》（The Net），一個擅長檢修遊戲軟體的電腦系統分析師安琪拉・班奈特，在測試一個電腦程式時，無意中接取到一份她不該取得的資料，因而把她的生活搞得天翻地覆。這部電影中所描述的安琪拉，舉凡工作、交友、購物等日常生活大小事宜，都在網路上解決。因為平常很少出門，所以連鄰居、朋友都無人見過她的面，以致後來她的身分被別人取代，卻沒有人可以為她作證，指認她就是她！當然，這樣的情節是有點誇張，但也不啻為對未來生活的一種警訊，提醒我們在使用電腦過生活的同時，不要忘記敦親睦鄰。

目前我們的工作環境是集中式辦公室，大家從不同的地方開車到公司來上班。但在多媒體工作環境之下，集中辦公室會演變成分散式辦公室。因為，如果多媒體可經由通訊網路傳輸，使我們在家裡就可以看到另外一個人，今天我們就不用去上班了。因為我們上班是為了辦事的，與同事們並不需要真正的身體接觸。

Tomorrow

明日工作室 策劃
溫世仁 監製

你能懂

2 小時掌握一個知性主題

半導體

It!

邢智田
劉叔慧 合著

You Got

沒有半導體，就沒有現代文明！

從會唱歌的生日賀卡、電子錶
到電腦、金融連線、生產線的運轉、保全系統
本書讓你明白什麼是半導體
半導體又是如何建構了現代文明……

Tomorrow

明日工作室 策劃

溫世仁 監製

蔡志忠
千禧蟲防治造型設計

你能懂

2小時掌握一個知性主題

千禧蟲危機

It!

鄒景平
張成華　合著

在千禧年來臨的前夕

取消你的旅遊計畫

確認你的銀行存款

準備足夠的現金和糧食

然後，趕快打開這本書！

You Got

Y2K

TIME

TIME

TIME

LOCUS

LOCUS

LOCUS

LOCUS